Harvard Historical Studies, Volume LXXXIV

Published under the direction of the
Department of History from the income
of the Henry Warren Torrey Fund.

A Mirror of England

ENGLISH PURITAN VIEWS OF
FOREIGN NATIONS, 1618-1640

by Marvin Arthur Breslow

HARVARD UNIVERSITY PRESS

Cambridge, Massachusetts, 1970

To My Parents

Acknowledgments

A grateful listing of the many obligations I have incurred in the research for and writing of this study does not lessen my responsibility for what is written, but it does seek to thank those who made my task easier.

My first research was done in Widener Library and the Houghton Library at Harvard University, and I particularly wish to express my debt to the late Professor William Jackson and the staff at the Houghton Library. Through the generosity of the General Research Board of the University of Maryland, I was able to conduct additional research in England. The Public Record Office and the British Museum were valuable sources of materials, and the Institute of Historical Research was a valuable source of hospitality. I am fortunate to be so near the Folger Shakespeare Library; and, although no known Jacobean incantation can transmute tea into coffee or win a fair parking place on Capitol Hill, Dr. Louis B. Wright and the able staff have done so much for me that I am a selfish and most enthusiastic admirer of the Folger.

Professor Glenn W. Gray, who introduced me to the study

of Stuart England when I was an undergraduate at the University of Nebraska, has continued to be generous of his time and knowledge. Professor Paul K. Conkin has done much to deepen my understanding of Puritanism. Professors Aubrey C. Land, David A. Shannon, and Francis C. Haber, each in his own way, gave me encouragement and support.

Mr. Stephen Goodell was my tyrannical typist, and Mr. Grant Stivers and Miss Michael Adler helped in many ways.

Finally and foremost, my debt to Professor W. K. Jordan is a pleasant burden. He directed my doctoral dissertation, and for his advice, kindness, and encouragement, then and later, I am sincerely grateful.

Marvin Arthur Breslow

College Park, Maryland
April 1969

Contents

A Mirror of England: English Puritan
Views of Foreign Nations, 1618-1640

ABBREVIATIONS

Birch, *Charles I*   Thomas Birch, *The Court and Times of Charles the First* (2 vols.; London, 1848)

Birch, *James I*   Thomas Birch, *The Court and Times of James the First* (2 vols.; London, 1848)

Chamberlain, *Letters* *The Letters of John Chamberlain,* ed. Norman E. McClure (Philadelphia, 1939)

CSPD, Charles I   *Calendar of State Papers, Domestic Series, of the Reign of Charles I*

CSPD, James I   *Calendar of State Papers, Domestic Series, of the Reign of James I*

D'Ewes   *The Autobiography and Correspondence of Sir Simonds D'Ewes, Bart., during the reigns of James I. and Charles I.,* ed. J. O. Halliwell (2 vols.; London, 1845)

Gardiner   S. R. Gardiner, *History of England from the Accession of James I. to the Outbreak of the Civil War, 1603–1642* (10 vols.; London, 1893–1899)

PRO SP 14   Public Record Office, State Papers Domestic, James I

PRO SP 16   Public Record Office, State Papers Domestic, Charles I

STC   *A Short-Title Catalogue of Books Printed in England, Scotland, & Ireland and of English Books Printed Abroad, 1475–1640,* comp. A. W. Pollard and G. R. Redgrave (2 vols.; London, 1926)

I

Introduction

The association between shrillest supernationalism and religious fervency is familiar in modern history. To state that Puritanism is a source of this association in the Anglo-American tradition would be only partially correct. If triumphant Puritanism had expressed itself in the rule of the major-generals but not in Milton, then the statement would be accurate. If the heirs of Puritanism were only the Bowdlers and the Comstocks but not the Gladstones and Emersons, then, too, the statement could stand uncorrected and whole. The Puritan reform impulse could have been reform rigidly imposed, or it could have been free reform that opposed coercion. Similarly, the part Puritanism played in forming a religious foundation for English nationalism contained an element that simplistically, stridently, called war holy, but another element in Puritan nationalism implied the necessity to judge and to criticize one's country and government. It is the intent of this study to describe and to analyze the Puritan contribution to English nationalism as it helped to shape the context of discontents in the decades before the English Revolution.

The suggestion for such a study is not new. In the beginning, more than a century ago, there was S. R. Gardiner: "It is seldom that events which have taken place upon the Continent have affected the course of English history so deeply as the struggle between the two religious parties in Germany which lit up the flames of the Thirty Years' War. The second growth of Puritanism, and the anti-monarchical feeling which reached its culminating point in the reign of Charles I., may be distinctly traced to the dissatisfaction of the nation with the desertion by James of his Protestant allies." [1] Nearly a century later the suggestion, more broadly framed, was renewed: "Nationalism in seventeenth-century England deserves far more scholarly attention than it has received: it may, indeed, constitute the most important element in the social consciousness that ended in revolution." [2]

The problem will be approached by considering the views of the English Puritans toward foreign nations at the time of the Thirty Years' War, for it is reasonable to expect that those Englishmen who, in their own statements, proclaimed their belief that they were the most truly Protestant part of English society would have strong opinions about the position they expected England to take in a war that appeared to be determining the future of Protestantism. Thus, the Puritans' attitudes toward the warring European nations also expressed aspects of their thinking about England, and in their views of foreign nations there was mirrored a view of England — a view that was employed to measure the religion and patriotism of Englishmen. This study will seek to demonstrate how, to the English Puritans, the flames of the Thirty Years' War were the fire in which their nationalism was refined.

1. *Letters and Other Documents Illustrating the Relations between England and Germany at the Commencement of the Thirty Years' War,* ed. S. R. Gardiner, Camden Society, XC (Westminster, 1865), Preface.

2. Charles H. George and Katherine George, *The Protestant Mind of the English Reformation, 1570–1640* (Princeton, 1961), 251.

During the first two decades of the Thirty Years' War, foreign affairs served as the issue out of which views about England were articulated; but during the preceding two generations men had labored to create new historical perceptions, and these formed the background for the later Puritan efforts. Even before the accession of Elizabeth a new history of religion in England was being pieced together. In its fullness the new history told Englishmen that Christianity had come to England before the Roman missionaries and that the seeds of pure Christianity had remained throughout the centuries of dominant Romanism. John Foxe and his fellows proclaimed England's religious independence, and their understanding was accepted by the more secular historians, such as William Camden.[3] With this historical perception of England's uniqueness as their background, the Puritans in the early seventeenth century were able to move towards a definition of England and Englishmen.

Before discussing the opinions of the English Puritans, it is necessary to make a few remarks about the holders of the opinions. In one sense this study reveals its own definition of "Puritan"; for, insofar as a pattern of thought can be found in the Puritan views of other nations, that pattern might be expected to provide some kind of definition of "Puritan." Unquestionably, such a definition would be circular within this study. For the purposes of this work, the identification of individual Puritans has proved more useful than a definition of "Puritan." [4] Whenever possible, the task of iden-

3. William Haller, *Foxe's Book of Martyrs and the Elect Nation* (London, 1963), 140–186, 224–250; F. J. Levy, "The Making of Camden's *Britannia*," *Bibliothèque d'Humanisme et Renaissance*, 26 (1964), 70–97. See also "The Norman Yoke," chap. 3 of Christopher Hill, *Puritanism and Revolution* (London, 1958), 50–122.

4. For some recent discussions see "The Definition of a Puritan," chap. 1 of Christopher Hill, *Society and Puritanism in Pre-Revolutionary England* (New York, 1964), 13–29; Basil Hall, "Puritanism: The Problem of Defini-

tification has been left to others, either to seventeenth-century sources or to modern scholarship.

A few of the men whose opinions are cited were, as far as can be learned, not Puritans. Their views have been used as illustrations of the views of the ordinary Protestant Englishman: the larger body of English public opinion. John Chamberlain, whose letters are extensive and informative, is the most frequently cited source for what can be described as the opinions of the informed, interested, Protestant Englishman. If anything, he represents the maximum general interest, for his position in London and his connections with the Carleton family make the degree of his interest atypical. Within Parliament, Puritan and non-Puritan critics are not easily distinguished. Prominent figures, such as Phelips, Seymour, and Coke, can serve as a base line of political opinion that was not necessarily Puritan.

Mention of these politically conscious Protestant Englishmen raises an important question about the Puritans: were there any significant differences between the attitudes of the Puritans and the general public? A partial answer to this question is that the English Puritans thought their views were different, when, as a matter of fact, the Protestant public seems to have had some of the same attitudes, although they were less clearly defined. The significant difference lay in the manner in which the attitudes were expressed. The differences were in degrees of intensity: the general public was usually more passive where foreign nations were concerned; their attitudes were usually vague feelings. In contrast, the Puritans were conscious, articulate, and vigorous, and those active qualities marked the Puritan efforts to educate, by means of pamphlet and sermon, their countrymen,

---

tion," *Studies in Church History*, II, 283–296, ed. G. J. Cuming (London, 1965); Charles H. George, "Puritanism in History and Historiography," *Past and Present*, 41 (December 1968), 77–104.

who more and more came to accept the stronger Puritan approach. Greater concern, greater clarity in seeing the issues, and the forcefully critical presentation of the issues are the significant distinctions between the English Puritans and the Protestant public. Chamberlain's letters showed an intelligent concern, but D'Ewes' diary showed his personal agonizings over the course of foreign affairs. The men who from pulpit and press defied James and Charles were men who were called, or who gloried in the name of, Puritan. This difference between zealous activity and interested passivity was the quality that most distinguished the Puritan approach and that makes their thinking important, for their expressions were the cutting edge of criticism that opened the way for others to follow.[5]

This study of Puritan views is set in the period of the Thirty Years' War, but it terminates eight years before the end of the war. The reasons for not proceeding beyond 1640 can be seen in the course of the war and in English domestic events. The Thirty Years' War was never solely a religious war, although it began and continued with the contestants generally divided into Protestant and Catholic camps. However, when the Swedish crusade for German Protestantism collapsed at Nordlingen, the survival of Protestantism in Germany became dependent upon the open support of Catholic France; and in 1635 the character of the war was clearly changing into a squabble for spoils among the petty impotencies which were caught in a Franco-Hapsburg war for the hegemony of Europe.

Even though this alteration in the character of the war might not have been immediately apparent to contemporary onlookers, the onlookers in England, at least, had other matters of increasing importance to absorb their interest and

5. Patrick Collinson, *The Elizabethan Puritan Movement* (London, 1967), 26–28. Collinson makes a similar point about Puritan theology.

5

energy. The outbreak of rebellion in Scotland wrecked any chance for English participation in the continental war; and as the Scottish crisis turned into an English one, all Englishmen were compelled to turn their gaze inward and to give their attention exclusively to English problems. It is likely that the turning inward was well advanced before 1637. The Parliament of 1628–29 was almost introspective, and after 1629 there was, of course, no Parliament to provide a public forum. In addition, Laud's efforts to control press and pulpit diminished the quantity of criticism. By the mid-1630's the realities of foreign affairs had been largely replaced by a myth of foreign policy, and this myth was also turned inward. By 1640 the war in Europe was not the war it had been, and England was absorbed in its own war and in itself. Hence, the events that by 1640 had forced changes in the viewpoints of Englishmen seem to provide sufficient reason for terminating this consideration of the English Puritans' views in that year.

Fortunately, the Puritans were verbal, and their views can be found in several types of materials. The parliamentary diaries are pertinent inasmuch as they are "live" reports on debates about foreign affairs. Letters and sermons are important, but some of the letter writers and some of the preachers seem to be exercising a caution born of the knowledge that letters and sermons were not always safe ways to voice critical opinions. The same objection does not apply to the polemic tract or to the diary and memoir sources. The diarists usually were free and candid in their observations and criticisms, while the polemicist, as long as he kept himself beyond the reach of government discipline, could be violent in his expressions. The only restraint on the fugitive pamphleteer was the self-restraint imposed by his desire to persuade the government or the influential groups, who at this time would not countenance disloyalty to the crown.

Unfortunately, the Puritan views were nowhere fully stated in any single source; no individual Puritan sat down and wrote out a comprehensive statement of those views. For the most part the views were embedded among other materials; most often they were in the form of comments of the moment, coming as reactions and responses to events. Among the Puritan ministers the leading figures, such as Sibbes, Gouge, and Preston, often veiled their comments in allusions. The less prominent were often the more outspoken, but even the most energetic Puritan propagandist, Thomas Scott, did not offer an elaborated conceptual approach of general applicability; he, too, was most concerned with the issue at hand, the immediate problem of a specific situation. Although the sources of the Puritan views were fragmentary, that does not mean that the Puritan views were fragmentary. On the contrary, the fragments compose themselves into recognizable patterns which reveal some fundamental propositions of Puritan thought.

A suitable manner in which to demonstrate the form of this Puritan thought is to display the Puritans' views about specific countries, for in that way documentation and analysis of each country's place can be presented, while also indicating the recurrence of the patterns of Puritan thought. To do this, four European countries — Germany, Spain, the Netherlands, and France — will be treated in the next five chapters. It may be useful here to offer a few preliminary remarks on each.

The Thirty Years' War began in Germany, and most of the fighting occurred in that area. For the English Puritans, the problem in Germany came to have two major focal points. First, their interest focused on the affairs of the Elector Palatine, his quest for the Bohemian Crown, and the subsequent disasters that nearly destroyed German Protestantism. The second point of focus came later when Gustavus Adolphus made his dramatic entrance into Germany to rescue the Protestants from their desperate condition. In order to keep a generally chronological sequence, the Puritan views on Germany are presented in two chapters; this convenient division should not be understood to mean that the question of the Palatinate was no longer of any importance to the Puritans after the appearance of Gustavus Adolphus, for the Palatinate remained unusually important to the English Puritans.

As for Spain, there should be little surprise concerning the place it occupied in Puritan thinking. English fear and hatred of Spain can be traced back to the mid-sixteenth century. During the first part of the Thirty Years' War, Spain appeared again as a dangerous and antagonistic force, capable of employing its dreaded armies in yet another drive for world dominion. To the English Puritans, however, the danger to England of Spanish trickery seemed fully as great as the danger from Spanish arms. So it was that, while anxiously aware of the Spanish military peril in Europe, the Puritans were most afraid of the Spanish conquest of England in 1624, the year of the proposed marriage of Prince Charles to the Infanta of Spain. Then the Puritan view of Spain was forcefully enunciated in the effort to awaken England to the Spanish threat.

The exposition of the Puritans' Dutch views, unlike the discussion of their attitudes toward Germany and Spain, cannot be centered on any particularly critical event. To the Puritans the greatest Dutch problem was the series of commercial irritations arising from Anglo-Dutch trade rivalry and creating, at the time of the massacre at Amboyna, strong reaction in England. Frequent frictions required special Puritan attention to England's relations with the United Provinces, but the frequency and variety of those conflicts produced a somewhat diffused picture which lacks the advantage of a focusing issue or event. Nevertheless, the Puritan effort to balance Anglo-Dutch alliance with Anglo-Dutch friction reveals many of the fundamentals of the total Puritan view.

It is equally important to consider the Puritans' attitude toward France, for here they were also faced with the task of comprehending conflicting interests. Here, too, the attempt to harmonize conflicting interests reveals more of the essentials of Puritan thought than is available in their attitudes toward those nations to which fairly simplistic views could be applied. The major difference between the Puritan views of France and the Netherlands is that for France the conflict of interests was realized in a crucial event, the siege of La Rochelle, and the Puritan position in regard to that event suggested the resolution to their seemingly contradictory approaches to France.

Following the analysis of Puritan views toward specific countries, the concluding chapter of this study is devoted to the construction of a coherent Puritan outlook. The pattern revealed in the views of individual countries is treated in terms of a Puritan image of England, and it is shown how the Puritan views of other nations, at the time of the Thirty Years' War, mirrored a view of England that in the Puritan mind served as a measurement by which the true Englishman could be identified. The Puritan examination of England and Englishmen articulated a sense of nationalism that was a factor in the Puritans' increased alienation from the royal leadership of England.[6]

6. Whether the Puritan criticisms were either accurate or valid is not relevant here. James, at least, may have had the better policies, but without a doubt the Puritans had the better propaganda.

II

The Palatinate

The Bohemian Crown

The election of Frederick V of the Palatinate to the Bohemian Crown in 1618 broke the fragile European peace and dashed Europe into a war of such destructive proportions that three centuries had to pass before a comparable war was waged. The Thirty Years' War, which was to engage the entire continent, never directly touched England, no foreign armies lived off the English countryside, and no English town was burned and sacked; but Englishmen were not aloof from the events across the channel. They were deeply interested.

Elizabeth, the wife of Frederick, was the sole English princess; and Frederick, as Elector Palatine, was the chief Calvinist prince of the Empire. A dynastic tie and a religious kinship operated to attract England's attention to a distant part of Europe. And one modern historian has suggested that the interest created by the happenings in 1618 served to intensify a general interest in politics in England.[1]

News from Bohemia dominated the news pamphlets. Certainly an eager public must have existed, for they accepted almost anything printed. Even a translation of a mild and legalistic apology to the Emperor from the Bohemian Estates (often translated "Parliament") found its way into print.[2]

Another pamphlet of 1619 gave a description of the departure of Frederick and Elizabeth from their seat at Heidelberg for Prague, where they were to receive the Crown of Bohemia. The author marked with approval the actions of Frederick in giving away his hunting dogs and in appearing for religious services and sermons. The whole work has a tone of militant Protestantism. Frederick and Elizabeth were not journeying to Prague; they were "Debora and Barak now alreadie on their march." [3] Their crusade, the author reminded the reader, had a special meaning for England: "And shall we suffer our sweete Princess, our royall infanta, the only daughter of our soveraigne lord and king, to goe before us into the field and not follow after her?" [4]

1. Godfrey Davies, "English Political Sermons, 1603–1640," *Huntington Library Quarterly*, 3 (October 1939), 4.

2. *Newes From Bohemia An Apologie Made by the States of the Kingdom of Bohemia* . . . (London, 1619). Also see: *The reasons wh. compelled the states of Bohemia to reject the archiduke Ferdinand* (Dort, 1619); *The Last newes from Bohemia* (n. p., 1620); *The Present state of the affairs betwixt the Emperor and King of Bohemia* (London [?], 1620). A further indication of interest is the fact that four newsletters on affairs in Germany are calendared within a ten-month period of the early 1620's in *Harley Letters and Papers*, Historical Manuscripts Commission, Fourteenth Report, Appendix, Part II: *The Manuscripts of His Grace The Duke of Portland, preserved at Welbeck Abbey*, III, 14–16.

3. John Harrison, *A Short Relation of the departure of the high and mightie Prince Frederick King Elect of Bohemia; with his royall & vertous Ladie Elizabeth: And the thryse hopefull young Prince Henrie, from Heydelberg towards Prague, to receiuse the Crowne of that Kingdome* (Dort, 1619), 3.

4. *Ibid.*, 4–5.

These pamphlets fed upon a strong interest in England in following the wild adventure of the Bohemian Crown. In 1620 a correspondent was grateful to Lord Zouch for the good news that John Hus and Jerome of Prague were being avenged by Frederick in Bohemia.[5] But there were some men in England who were not satisfied simply to follow the news: there were those who wanted to act.

To Englishmen concerned with the struggle in Bohemia and the cause represented by Frederick and Elizabeth, two lines of action presented themselves: money and arms were seen as the ways in which the individual could participate. In April of 1620 John Chamberlain, the best gossip in London, wrote to Sir Dudley Carleton and described for him some of the fund raising for Bohemia. The City officials were "about some course to provide monie for Bohemia" and "there is a collection likewise among the Clergie, wherof divers have underwritten bountifully and cherefully." A specific case that Chamberlain related was that of the Earl of Dorset, who had contributed £1000 and promised to give that sum annually for the next four years.[6] Others responded by taking up arms to fight for religion and the Bohemian Crown. One old earl addressed himself to King James and expressed his readiness to serve the royal daughter with the hope of seeing her become Empress.[7] And to those who went to the war John Taylor offered a ten-page patriotic poem in which he recited the warlike qualities of the English and Scots. That their victory was assured seemed clear to Taylor, who wrote to the soldiers:

> Since God then in his love did preordaine
> That you should be his Champions, to maintaine

5. PRO SP 14/113/77.
6. Chamberlain, *Letters*, 300.
7. *The Fortescue Papers*, ed. S. R. Gardiner, Camden Society, n.s., I (Westminster, 1871), 141.

His quarrell, and his cause; a fig for foes,
God being with you, how can man oppose?[8]

Excited interest, and aid in the form of money and men, did not long keep the Bohemian Crown on the head of the Elector Palatine. The defeat at White Mountain lost him Bohemia, and more defeats robbed the luckless prince of his own patrimony. But it was at this point that two Puritan ministers published justifications of Frederick's claims to Bohemia. Thomas Scott wrote a sixty-page tract made up of legal and historical arguments in support of the sometime King of Bohemia;[9] and Alexander Leighton, writing on the just war, devoted a chapter to the defense of Frederick's true election to the Bohemian Crown.[10]

Although Leighton's concern was to demonstrate the legality of the Elector's actions, he was not blind to what had happened; and he went on to suggest that there had been a lack of preparation and diligence.[11] Later Scott, when he was desperate to have England at war with Spain, was prepared to abandon Bohemia and his views on the Bohemian Crown. He addressed himself to King James: "Although it be true, that the Prince Palatyne your Son-in-law, committed a first errour of Estate, in assuming and taking on him the Crowne of Bohemia . . . You likewise sawe and suffered the Emperour to chastice him from Bohemia; and therein you shewed an act of Justice, which celebrates your fame to

8. John Taylor, *A Friendly Farewell to all the noble Souldiers that goe out of Great Britaine unto Bohemia* (n. p., 1620), 2–3.

9. Thomas Scott, *A Briefe Information of the Affaires of the Palatinate* (n. p., 1624).

10. A[lexander] L[eighton], *Speculum Belli sacri: or the Lookingglasse of the Holy War* (n. p., 1624), chap. 3. This was dedicated to Frederick and Elizabeth.

11. *Ibid.,* 150.

all Europe . . ." [12] A final word on the Bohemian Crown came in 1628, when the Palatinate as well as Bohemia seemed to be lost. The poet-polemicist author of *The Spy* stated that Frederick's election had been a Jesuit device to trap him and confuse England.[13]

When arms and money could not keep Frederick and Elizabeth in Prague, when patriotic poems and legal arguments could not produce a crusade for Bohemia, then the quest from its beginning had to be attributed to a devil. The Bohemian Crown was no longer a political reality even for the extreme Protestants in England, but the war that had begun for Bohemia now endangered Protestantism everywhere in Germany. Here was a new cause.

The Distressed Church in Germany

The failure of the Elector Palatine was a triumph for Hapsburg Catholicism and a disaster for German Protestantism. In England part of the response to the quest for the Bohemian Crown had been political and military action to support an adventure which initially had promised to forward Protestantism. Now the response to the perils of Protestantism was essentially a feeling of sympathy.

The basis for such a response, especially from the Puritans, was their sense of fellowship in one Church which included their religious brethren in Germany. John Preston, perhaps the most influential Puritan preacher of his day, expounded a large view of the Church. To him the Protestant cause everywhere was one, and he spoke in terms of churches or peoples rather than in terms of states. Naturally, he was

---

12. S. R. N. I. [Thomas Scott], *Votivae Angliae: Or, The Desires And Wishes of England* (Utrecht, 1624), sig. A1v.

13. J. R., *The Spy Discovering the Danger of Arminian Heresie and Spanish Trecherie* (Strasburgh, 1628), sig. B2.

troubled by the weakening of international Calvinism, engaged in a struggle for Christ but losing to Antichrist.[14] With explicit identification of those in the "fellowship of the spirit," Alexander Leighton passionately wrote in favor of "your mournfull sisters Bohemia, and the Palatinate."[15] Thomas Gataker, another Puritan minister, addressed the company of lawyers at Sergeants Inn with questions posed to move sympathetic responses: "Can we heare daily reports of our brethren in foraine parts, either assaulted, or distressed, or surprised by Popish forces, and a main breach made into the state of those that are by bonds, civill and sacred, so nearely knit to us, and yet esteeme all is nothing, or thinke that we have no just cause to mourne and lament? Neither let any man say; What is their affliction to us? What are those parts to these? What is France or Germanie to England? For What was Jerusalem to Antioch? What was Judah to Joseph?"[16] And Thomas Scott reminded King James that he was styled Defender of the Faith, and that the German Protestants, being of that same faith, needed to be defended.[17]

Not all of the Reformed Churches in Germany merited the sympathy of the English Puritans. The Lutherans were described as less orthodox than the Protestants of the Helvetic and Belgic confessions. Also, the Lutherans under John George of Saxony had been guilty of aiding the Catholics in their persecutions "of the more orthodox Protestants of Germany."[18]

14. Christopher Hill, *Puritanism and Revolution* (London, 1958), 249–251. See *The New Life*, 49–53, and *A sensible Demonstration of the Deity*, 84, in John Preston, *Sermons Preached Before his Majestie; and upon other speciall occasions* (London, 1630), a collection of five sermons published posthumously and edited by Thomas Goodwin and Thomas Ball.

15. Leighton, *Speculum Belli sacri*, 3–4.

16. Thomas Gataker, *A Sparke Toward the Kindling of Sorrow for Sion* (London, 1621), 32–33.

17. Scott, *Votivae Angliae*, sig. B1v.

18. D'Ewes, I, 259.

The sympathy English Puritans felt for their coreligionists was not simply a sympathy produced by a similarity of ideals. It could take an agonizingly personal form. Sir Simonds D'Ewes wrote on the defeats of 1620: "Most sad and doleful were these tidings to all true Protestant hearts in England, each able judgment fearing that it would, in the end, draw with it the utter and general subversion of God's true Church." And when by 1626 his fears had proved true, he lamented: "And yet I was not so much dejected nor troubled with all my private pressures and grievances, as I was afflicted and sometimes affrighted with the public calamities and daily subversion of God's dear Church and children abroad; which were sometimes hastened, if not occasioned by our miseries and divisions here at home."[19] God's Church, of which the Calvinist Churches in Germany were members, was afflicted by Antichrist, and to that affliction the Puritan responded from his sense of sympathetic fellowship with feelings of personal identification.

In England the sympathy for the collapse of Calvinism in Germany was enforced with a substantial dose of horror. For the writers of the time, it was not always sufficient to write about the loss of Protestant territories through political and military defeats; they also described the losses of individual professors of true religion. These civilians were never killed; they were horribly butchered after inhuman torturing of the men and shameful abuse of the women.[20]

The sight of the Church reeling and the literary screams of tortured believers gave rise to more than sympathy and horror. Some in England felt a burden of guilt; they saw sinful England cursed for not having done more for the distressed Church abroad.[21] A frivolous court was marked for

19. *Ibid.*, I, 153, 323.
20. Leighton, *Speculum Belli sacri*, 182–183.
21. Gataker, *A Sparke Toward the Kindling of Sorrow for Sion*, 33. See

having mocked the Puritans who would fast and pray "when the Church of God is in so great affliction in Bohemia and Germany . . ." [22] And a worried member of Parliament saw England punished for this sin when he observed: "itt is true that the state of the Country in the encrease of Cattell and commodities hath beene of late not soe happie as in former times: the cause hee takes to bee want of assistance to the professors of the gospell that suffred for want of our releife: if this cause cease through gods mercy itt will bee blest agen." [23]

There were, however, some actions available to the person moved by the appeals for the brethren in Germany. Perhaps the most usual form of assistance was prayer. A Puritan minister with General Vere's forces wrote letters, which were published in a pamphlet; he concluded with this prompting: "Thus beseeching God to blesse you with all yours, and praying you to stirre up all the prayers you can for the distressed people of God here, and even for our troupers, and for me, that I may do the greate worke of God faithfully and fruitfully in this emploiment . . ." [24]

---

also the collection of twenty of Gataker's sermons and meditations, *Certaine Sermons, First Preached, And After Published at severall times* (London, 1637), especially *David's Remembrancer*, in part I, 333, 343, and *Noah His Obedience*, in part II, 4–5.

22. Birch, *James I*, II, 227–228.

23. Sir John Walter in the House of Commons on 19 March 1624, Gurney Manuscript, "Parliament Debates 1624," 134.

24. J. B., *Certaine letters declaring in part the passage of affaires in the Palatinate* (Amsterdam, 1621). J. B. was probably John Burgess. Internal evidence suggests that he was a minister; and another pamphlet — A. M., *A Relation of the Passages of our English Companies* (London, 1621), 4 — mentions that a Dr. John Burgess was with the English soldiers. "Master Doctor Burges, now Preacher to the English troops in the Pallatinate," published Thomas Clarke's *The Popes deadly Wound* (London, 1621). Finally, the *DNB* identifies a Puritan minister, John Burgess, who went with Vere to the Palatinate.

Charity, too, was a form of action, and the Puritan ministers gained results when they urged contributions for the unfortunate of the true religion. In 1627 Thomas Taylor, Richard Sibbes, John Davenport, and William Gouge wrote a circular letter in which they called upon "all godly Christians" to raise a supply for the relief of 240 preachers and several thousand others of the Upper Palatinate. More than £1750 was collected. So successful were these Puritan ministers that government officials feared that charity for the German Protestants was being more willingly subscribed than the forced loan.[25]

Preaching could prompt other than charitable actions. One such action betrayed frustration in England over the events in Germany. Secretary of State Calvert wrote to Buckingham that, as a result of pamphlets, pasquils, and "factious sermons preached in many pulpitts about London," the Spanish Ambassador was in personal danger.[26] Violence was done in London to avenge the violence done to the distressed Church in Germany.

The Unnatural Father

"Yea, what would not England doe for my dear and Royall Sister of Bohemia, if the King my Father would but give it the word of command?" These words were imputed by Thomas Scott to the late Prince Henry in a celestial debate over the foreign policy of England.[27] Implied was the belief

25. PRO SP 16/64/11; *CSPD, Charles I,* III, 406; Gardiner, VII, 261.

26. *The Fortescue Papers,* 144–145. Horton Davies, *The Worship of the English Puritans* (Glasgow, 1948) 196, explains the effectiveness of the Puritan sermon: since it was meant for edification, its author sought to make it memorable to his audience of zealous members, who were expected to study it.

27. [Thomas Scott], *Vox Coeli, or Newes From Heaven* (Elisium [Utrecht?], 1624), 47.

that England's inaction, while the Bohemian Crown was being lost and the Church in Germany was being distressed, was the fault of King James. James became one point of focus for the English discontent which arose as a reaction to the parlous situation of Protestantism in Europe.

James had disapproved of Frederick's acceptance of the Bohemian Crown, and even when his son-in-law was under attack he did not act. Those in England interested in Bohemia tried to press King James to take effective action, and these attempts at pressure were reported in 1620 by the ambassadors of the United Provinces and the Republic of Venice. The Venetian wrote that "the whole nation takes the same side, and all the kingdom declares its impatience of this prolonged irresolution." [28] Later a Puritan writer asserted that "the Sanctuary of the Lord," the Palatinate, would not have been desecrated had James moved to hinder Spinola.[29] In a poem attributed to Scott, James was accused of being satisfied that Frederick should have lands and life.[30] When nothing could be gained from the King, Leighton turned to address himself to the public, to Parliament, and to "the Hope of great Brittain," Prince Charles, whose support for the Palatinate and the cause of religion was solicited.[31]

Some Englishmen, however, tried to find an explanation for the King's unpopular stance. There were those who traced

28. *Letters and Other Documents Illustrating the Relations between England and Germany at the Commencement of the Thirty Years' War,* ed. S. R. Gardiner, Camden Society, 2d ser., XCVIII (Westminster, 1868), 142, 148; *Tom Tell-Troath* (1622), in *Somers Tracts,* ed. Sir Walter Scott (13 vols.; London, 1809–1815), II, 471–472.

29. Leighton, *Speculum Belli sacri,* 180.

30. [Thomas Scott?], *The Interpreter* (n. p., 1622), 7–8. The *STC* suggests that this is perhaps by Scott, and for the lack of definite evidence to the contrary that authorship has been accepted here. Certainly the point of view is typical of Scott; however, this would then be the sole pamphlet of 1624 or earlier which was not included in *The Workes.*

31. Leighton, *Speculum Belli sacri,* first preface.

the fault to Spanish influence, but they were divided into two schools. The first group was willing to believe that James himself had been duped by Spain's (usually Gondomar's) false promises.[32] The second group thought the King had been ill advised by some members of the Council who either were pro-Spanish or were in the pay of Spain.[33] Neither explanation really removed the focus of blame from the sovereign.

More damaging to the royal reputation was the charge that James was an unnatural father. Into this charge were gathered many of the frustrations over the Bohemian Crown and the Church in Germany that had exercised elements in England.

The bond of royal blood united Englishmen with the Elector's family. When the birth of a child to that family was not celebrated in England, the omission was remarked on with a slighting reflection on James.[34] A Puritan accused James of dishonoring the royal son-in-law by denying the titles of Count and Elector to him.[35] The same writer, in another work, told James that in the number of his heirs — Charles, Elizabeth, and her children — he, James, was protected from Jesuit plots against his life.[36] Thus the father was assured of safety, though he would do nothing for the safety of his own children.

Another bond between England and the afflicted in Germany was religion. When a famine in Spain seemed to aid the German Protestants, a Puritan diarist commented that

32. PRO SP 14/112/10; J. R., *The Spy*, sig. B2v.

33. PRO SP 14/110/81; Chamberlain, *Letters*, 412. Chamberlain reported with approval a speech by John Pym. J. R., *The Spy*, sigs. D3-D4v.

34. Chamberlain, *Letters*, 284–285.

35. Scott, *Votivae Angliae*, sig. A3.

36. [Thomas Scott], *Vox Dei* (n. p., 1624), 84–85; Scott, *Votivae Angliae*, sig. C1v.

"thus God fighteth for his church when others neglect it." [37]
Scott employed the ghost of the Earl of Essex to tell the
English nobility to rouse their King, for "the blood of the
Saints doth continually cry at Heaven gates for Venge-
ance." [38] Apparently, the blood of the martyrs in Germany
was upon the royal head in England.

The most violent criticism of the King was made by
Thomas Barnes in a pamphlet in which by implication the
King was portrayed as a cursed ruler of the type represented
by Saul. Barnes stated that his call to write *Vox Belli* came
from God, and he hoped that his book might "prevaile to
provoke them whom it concernes, to a readinesse to succour
the destressed Church in forreine parts." [39] His fearful text
was Jeremiah 48:10: " 'Cursed be he that keepeth backe his
sword from bloud.' " And his point was made when he
wrote on the duty of the Christian magistrate in war: "When
a Christian Prince, partly to preserve the lives, liberties, and
religion of his owne subjects; partly to relieve his Allies
abroad, which are neere unto him, both in the flesh and in the
Lord, when they are oppressed by the common adversary,
shall make warre, it is not onely lawfull, but also needefull,
that did hee not doe it, he should highly displease God, as
being an unnatural father to his country, & an unkind friend
to them, whom hee doth owe, and should shew most kinde-
nesse unto." [40]

The King of England, the unnatural father, would not act

37. *Diary of Walter Yonge, Esq. from 1604 to 1628,* ed. George Roberts,
Camden Society, XLI (London, 1848), 59.

38. [Thomas Scott], *Robert Earle of Essex His Ghost, Sent from Elizian:
To The Nobility, Gentry, And Communaltie Of England* (Paradise [Lon-
don], 1624), 17.

39. Thomas Barnes, *Vox Belli, Or An Alarum To Warre* (London, 1626),
second page of Epistle Dedicatory.

40. *Ibid.,* 31.

to lead the nation where many felt it must go. On earth was there any place left to which they might hopefully appeal? They thought there was such a court. There was Parliament.[41]

The Failure of Parliament

There was Parliament, and Parliament was a place in which to air opinions and a place which offered opportunities for action. Here grievances could be redressed; here the hopes in England for the cause of the Palatinate could be expressed with confidence that something would be done.

For the Puritans, Parliament was coming to have a particular importance. Their desires for religious reformation had not been satisfied by King or Convocation, or by earlier Parliaments, but Parliament still stood as a possible opening to further reformation. Although the preachers, the natural Puritan leaders, could not serve as members of Commons, their influence could be directed toward the lay Puritan members and those other members who were in agreement on many issues with Puritanism, which was to become more and more identified with an uncompromising, militant Protestantism. John Preston's biographer and editor, Thomas Ball, remarked that Preston valued the lectureship at Lincoln's Inn, where he was assured an audience of Parliament men.[42] The Puritan in Parliament was, at least in the eyes of other Puritans, a member not like others; he was the honest, bold

---

41. *Letters and Other Documents of the Thirty Years' War,* XCVIII, 166.
42. Thomas Ball, *The Life of the Renowned Doctor Preston,* ed. E. W. Harcourt (Oxford, 1885), 60, 77; J. F. Maclear, "The Influence of the Puritan Clergy on the House of Commons, 1625–1629," *Church History,* 14 (December 1945), 272–273; W. K. Jordan, *The Development of Religious Toleration in England* (4 vols.; Cambridge, Mass., 1932–1940), II, 97–100; Michael Walzer, *The Revolution of the Saints: A Study in the Origins of Radical Politics* (Cambridge, Mass., 1965), 136–143, 257–263.

patriot, in contrast to the court sycophant and the timid timeserver.[43]

The Puritans could bring into Parliament an heroic image of themselves; they could bring there for resolution their hopes and frustrations for the Palatinate, which generally meant Calvinism in Germany; but all that they brought with them into Parliament must be weighed against what they really did for the Palatinate in five parliaments.

1621

The Palatinate received almost immediate attention in the Parliament of 1621 — the first since the brief, unhappy meeting in 1614. On 30 January, King James addressed Parliament and devoted much of his speech to an explanation of his policy: if he could not preserve Frederick by means of treaties, he would do it by war, but to do this he must have financial support from Parliament.[44] Action was swift. Although a few members opposed the voting of subsidies at the beginning of a session, the arguments for religion and the Palatinate swayed Commons enough so that on 15 February a committee of the whole House agreed to provide an immediate grant of two subsidies.[45]

At the same time that Commons was advancing money to assist the cause of religion abroad, it became incensed over an incident in its own House. The religious temper of Commons can be gauged by its reactions to Shepherd's speech and its handling of the case of Edward Floyd a few months later. Shepherd attacked a Sabbath measure as a device of Puritan troublemakers. His statements produced a strong reaction, and when Pym delivered a vigorous denunciation of

43. Scott, *The Interpreter*, 5.
44. *Commons Debates for 1621,* ed. Wallace Notestein, Frances Helen Relf, and Hartley Simpson (7 vols.; New Haven, 1935), II, 9–11, 13n. This part of the speech was circulated to the public.
45. *Ibid.,* II, 84–92

him, Shepherd was judged to have forfeited his seat in Commons.[46]

The famous and complicated case of Edward Floyd began when Floyd, a Catholic prisoner in the Fleet, made some slanderous remarks about the Elector and Electress Palatine. A fellow prisoner alleged: "Floud sayed to him he hard that Prauge was taken and that Goodwife Pallsgrave and goodman Pallsegrave have taken ther heeles and were runn away, and that goodwife Pallsegrave was taken prisoner, as he heard." On 1 May the Commons debated these slanders, and proposals for Floyd's punishment were freely offered. However, what began as a show of loyalty to the cause of the Palatine family turned into a dispute with King and Lords over the jurisdiction of the Commons in such a case. The original purpose was lost in later debate, and Floyd's case became another fight by the House for what it considered to be its privileges.[47] In Commons the issue was clouded, but a Puritan diarist applauded the Commons when he wrote: "These days' actions I have added a little before the due time, that I might at once finish the relation of this business; in which the faithful, zealous affection of the whole state and kingdom, in their body representative, consisting of the two Houses of Parliament, was fully expressed to that royal Princess, our King's only daughter, amidst the many scorns and oppressions of her irreconcilable and bloody enemies." [48]

Generally, foreign affairs, even the Palatinate, received scant notice in the first five months of the Parliament of 1621. Not until James announced his intention of adjourning them, did the members again bring up the gravity of foreign affairs. When on 29 May James announced a terminal date,

46. *Ibid.,* IV, 52–53, 62–65, V, 499–503, 513; Gardiner, IV, 33–34.

47. *Commons Debates 1621,* III, 116–128. According to this account by Thomas Barrington, a Puritan country gentleman, over forty speakers suggested punishments for Floyd.

48. D'Ewes, I, 190.

there were speeches full of passion. The next day discussion was more extensive, and Sir Robert Phelips was the major speaker. He told them: "The King hath taken wayes, which I pray God he be not deceived in. The Children of the King are in a miserable estate, releived by other charyty; and I came with a resolution to have had somewhat donn for ther reestablishment and that we might not spend sommer upon sommer in speculation of ther miseries withoute redress. Can it be for the honor of England to receive such a wound . . . and shall we suffer the Kings Children to be kept upon charyty and not releive them. We want not men, mony, harts for this, lett us thinke then how to doe it." [49] The fruits of that thinking became known on 4 June, the date of adjournment. Commons approved with wild acclamation a resolution declaring that if the King's diplomatic efforts for the Palatinate failed, it would concur in his pledge to venture life and treasure for the recovery of the Palatinate and the restoration of his children.[50] Then it was adjourned. There remained for the Palatinate the Commons' declaration — its enthusiastic declaration.

Parliament reconvened in late November, and a great debate on foreign affairs was the first important business before the Commons. This debate actually was initiated by the King and his ministers, whose diplomatic efforts had been wrecked by the invasion of the Lower Palatinate. On 22 November Sir Edward Coke reviewed for the Commons the speeches made in the House of Lords by the Lord Keeper Williams, by Lord Digby, who had delivered an important relation on foreign affairs, and by Lord Treasurer Cranfield, who had given a financial report. Those speeches represented an effort to gain funds for the Palatinate.[51]

49. *Commons Debates 1621*, III, 345–352.
50. *Ibid.*, II, 428–429.
51. *Ibid.*, II, 432–439, III, 414–426.

The debate on 26 November was begun by Sir Dudley Digges, who viewed Europe as two great camps divided along religious lines, with Spain as head of the Catholics and England as head of the Reformed. He favored war for the Palatinate and also some diversion to weaken Spain.[52]

Digges soon was followed by Sir Robert Phelips, who seems to have been the most prominent "popular" leader on foreign affairs. He reviewed the conditions of the states of Europe, and then he considered the fallen estate of England, which, in turn, led him to remark on the Palatinate: "It pleased God to give England a croune of honor; and, had we kept that, I thinke we had kept the ballance of all Christendom on our side, and this we might have donn with as much right, nationall or religious, as may be, but stayed not heear." The Palatinate was lost, and England with its internal danger and unredresed grievances was financially exhausted. Phelips then proposed that they content themselves with the unprecedented two subsidies they had offered at the beginning, make this a session, and consider on war when they met again.[53] Apparently, the enthusiastic offers of May and June were not to stand in November.

Phelips' remarks did not pass without opposition from Secretary Calvert, who explained that the Reformed German princes would support action if England would supply them. He observed that it had been this Parliament which had urged James to unsheath his sword, but the King could not perform their wish without their help.[54]

Nevertheless, it was the proposals of Phelips which merited the approval of most of the speakers when debate was resumed the next day. John Pym was typical of those who

52. *Ibid.*, III, 445–447.
53. *Ibid.,* 450–452.
54. *Ibid.*, 453–454.

thought that England could not engage in a land war for the Palatinate until there was provision for greater security at home. Finally, after the same points with only minor variations had been belabored by several speakers, the great debate on foreign affairs waned as the House went on to discuss the appointment of a committee.[55]

On 28 November Pym presented for the consideration of the Commons an address on religion to the King. This embodied his suggestions from the preceding day's debate. Sir Edward Coke reported the resulting petition out of committee on 3 December. The petition contained a disastrous item on the marriage of the Prince of Wales, for when this item was passed it embroiled the members with the King in another long wrangle about their privileges.[56] A last-minute attempt to rescue something for the Palatinate came from the House of Lords, where Lord Digby, over the opposition of the Puritan Lord Saye, was permitted to give another narration to the Commons on the critical situation in Europe.[57] Commons, however, was now too much taken up by its dispute with James to act for the Palatinate. He resolved the conflict by dissolving the Parliament of 1621, which had talked much about the Palatinate but had done little for it.

1624

When a new Parliament assembled in 1624, it convened in an atmosphere of joy and expectation. Those feelings were epitomized by Thomas Scott, who began one of his pamphlets with "the shouts and acclamations of all true-hearted English" for the return of Prince Charles from Spain, ending

55. *Ibid.*, 459–473.
56. *Ibid.*, II, 461–469, 487–499.
57. Henry Elsing, *Notes of the Debates in the House of Lords . . . 1621*, ed. S. R. Gardiner, Camden Society, CIII (Westminster, 1870), 121–123.

the same piece with a hopeful address to the Parliament.[58] Another Puritan, Alexander Leighton, raised the expectation to an exalted plane, for he saw the Parliament assembled by means of divine providence to perform in England a new covenant before the Lord in the manner of David and Israel at Hebron.[59]

As Parliament was compared to the gathering of Israel at Hebron, so too there was for the Puritans a contemporary equivalent to King David. The position was not assigned to the failing King James, but rather to Prince Charles and the favorite Buckingham, with the latter as main initiator. For, as the Spanish Agent in London warned James, it was Buckingham who had pushed for the Parliament, that he might gain popular support from the Puritans.[60] The Spaniard was not wrong. Through the agency of Puritan preachers, such as Preston, Buckingham had formed in the Parliament a popular alliance which was enthusiastic for his foreign policy.[61]

Opposed to the stance of Buckingham and the Puritans was King James. Inclined to pacifism and abhorrent of a religious war, the King was persuaded to countenance a war; but he maintained that a war for the Palatinate must be directly for the Palatinate. Such a war would be a land war in Germany for the political purpose of restoring Frederick to his hereditary territory. James seems to have had some support in the House of Lords, where in the early days of this Parliament several peers agreed that an English army must

58. [Thomas Scott], *The Second Part of Vox Populi, or Gondomar appearing in the likenes of Matchiavell in a Spanish Parliament* (Goricom, 1624), 59–60. See also PRO SP 14/159/28.

59. Leighton, *Speculum Belli sacri,* second and third pages of address "To the Honorable and High Court of Parliament."

60. *CSPD, James I,* XI, 231.

61. J. F. Maclear, "Puritan Relations with Buckingham," *Huntington Library Quarterly,* 21 (February 1958), 111–115; Ball, *The Life of Preston,* 66–67.

go and restore the Palatinate to its lord.[62] Curiously, D'Ewes too expressed a similar hope for direct action when he wrote: "All men now seeing the treaty of the Spanish match and the peaceable restitution of the Palatinate broken off, verily hoped to see that recovered and the Gospel again settled in Germany by the armies and assistances of the King of Great Britain." [63]

In Parliament itself quite a different view prevailed. There, reigning as the popular leader in the brief hour of harmony with the Puritans, was the Duke of Buckingham with his newly found anti-Spanish policy, which he, the Prince, and others enunciated to the Parliament in their narration on the Spanish match. When the time came for the Commons to consider the issues, the lead was taken by the first speaker, Sir Benjamin Rudyerd, who now was the principal "popular" spokesman on foreign affairs in that body. The policy exposed in that first speech was to be the policy of the Commons throughout the session. Rudyerd argued that the marriage treaty must be broken off, for the negotiations over it had caused the Palatinate to be lost. Then he pointed out that "if we break off the treaty we must go make good the breach, we must maintain it and the likeliest way is by a war, which is the manlier and more english way." But to Rudyerd and those who spoke after him — Phelips, Fleetwood, Seymour, Eliot — the "english way" to war for the Palatinate was to make a diversion near at hand. The diversion was Spain.[64] Outside Westminster this idea that the Palatinate

62. Gardiner, V, 185–209; Henry Elsing, *Notes of the Debates in the House of Lords . . . 1624 and 1626*, ed. S. R. Gardiner, Camden Society, n.s., XXIV (Westminster, 1879), 5–9.

63. D'Ewes, I, 242.

64. Gurney MS, "1624," 44–46, 50, 54–61; Winchilsea Manuscript, "Parliament Diary of John Pym for 1624," fols. 10v–11v; D. H. Willson, *The Privy Councillors in the House of Commons, 1604–1629* (Minneapolis, 1940), 160–168.

could be effectively assisted by an English attack on Spain was echoed; and Scott, who in 1624 was at his zenith as a pamphleteer, specifically addressed the Parliament to that end.[65] Duke, Prince, Parliament, and propagandist were in accord for war against Spain.

For its version of the war policy the Parliament was not remiss in providing money. On 11 March, Rudyerd again led the way when he told his colleagues that they must not be staggered by the amounts required to implement their own advice. And in the same discussion Sir Edward Coke made the proposed war look like a profitable investment when he claimed that England prospered from its wars with Spain.[66] Coke's claim was not unique. Scott dedicated to this Parliament a pamphlet, the theme of which was identical with that of Coke's speech; and Scott — in his own name, through the ghost of the Earl of Essex, and in a pretended speech by Sir Edward Cecil — admonished the Parliament in three more pamphlets of the same year to be generous in support for the war.[67] When the Commons had assurance that the war would be prosecuted against Spain and that the money would be husbanded carefully, the fairly substantial sum of three subsidies and three fifteenths was offered.[68]

After making financial provision for a war with Spain, the Parliament occupied itself in meeting demands that England must be secured internally from the alleged subversion of the recusants. Identifying prominent Catholics and peti-

65. Scott, *Vox Coeli*, dedication.

66. Gurney MS, "1624," 100-108; Winchilsea MS, "1624," fol. 25-25v.

67. [Thomas Scott], *The Belgick Souldier: Dedicated to the Parliament. Or, Warre was a Blessing* (Dort, 1624), 2, 4-5, 14; Scott, *Votivae Angliae*, sig. D4v; Scott, *Essex His Ghost*, 16; [Thomas Scott], *A Speech Made In The Lower House of Parliament, By Sir Edward Cicell, Colonell* (London, 1624), 5.

68. Winchilsea MS, "1624," fols. 32v-33v; Gurney MS, "1624," 124-151.

tioning James for a stricter enforcement of the laws against recusants now became a major concern.[69]

Thus, by means of a diversion against Spain and more stringent controls over the Catholics in England, the Parliament of 1624 sought to help the distressed brethren in Germany.

1625

In many ways the first Parliament of King Charles was similar to the last Parliament of King James. For the purposes of the King and the favorite, however, the Parliament of 1625 was not enough like that of 1624. Charles and Buckingham, apparently unaware that their leadership in the previous meeting was more a result of their leading where Parliament wanted to go than of Parliament blindly following them, dissipated much of their goodwill. Still supremely confident of themselves, they made inadequate efforts to construct an effective Court party in the Commons.[70]

In the Parliament itself, immediate identification was made with the preceding Parliament when the problems of religion, which had exercised members in the final days of 1624, became the first major issue in 1625: "They begin to mutter about matters of religion . . . Some spare not to say that all goes backward since this connivance in religion came in, both in our wealth, honour, valour, and reputation, and that it is visibly seen God blesses nothing that we take in hand." [71] Shortly after the session began, John Preston preached

69. Winchilsea MS, "1624," 44v–45, 47–47v; *Debates in the House of Lords 1624 and 1626*, 53–57; [Thomas Scott], *Vox Regis* (n. p., 1624), 19–24. [Thomas Scott], *Boanerges. Or The Humble Supplication Of The Ministers Of Scotland, To The High Court Of Parliament In England* (Edinburgh, 1624), 20.

70. Willson, *The Privy Councillors*, 201–204.

71. Birch, *Charles I*, I, 36.

before Commons; his sermon emphasized the need for prayer and personal reformation in a time of plague. Vaguely and briefly touching on religion abroad, he declined to prescribe "unto you any particular direction," leaving the matter to the members own care.[72] When the Commons met in committee to consider the state of religion in England, care for the Palatinate indirectly entered the discussion, for "the distressed estate of the professors of our religion in forrayne partes" and "the unfortunate accedentes to the Princes nearest in blood to his Majestie" were named as causes of the increase of popery within England. The members of Commons proposed to fight this danger by means of better law enforcement and through reform in the Church of England.[73]

From the King, through his officials, came an appeal to Parliament to do something for the Palatinate in the Palatinate. The appeal took the line that if Parliament failed to subsidize the army of Count Mansfield then England would be forced to abandon the religious brethren in Germany and seek a peace disgraceful to the honor and safety of England and true religion. Later, to emphasize the seriousness of the request, the King personally addressed the members when they reassembled at Oxford in August.[74]

Even the King could not move this balky Parliament, which had grown increasingly suspicious of Buckingham's delusions of adequacy. It refused to give additional money for the Palatinate. On 5 August Sir Francis Seymour, Sir Robert

72. John Preston, *A Sermon Preached at a Generall Fast before the Commons-House of Parliament: the second of July, 1625,* in Preston, *The Saints Qualifications,* ed. Richard Sibbes and John Davenport (London, 1633), 293–294.

73. *Debates in the House of Commons in 1625,* ed. S. R. Gardiner, Camden Society, n.s., VI (Westminster, 1873), 18–27.

74. *Ibid.,* 56–59, 73–77; Sir John Eliot, *Negotium Posterorum,* in *An Apology for Socrates and Negotium Posterorum,* ed. A. B. Grosart (2 vols.; London, 1881), I, 114–117, II, 16–21.

Phelips, and Sir Edward Coke, who must have been the objectors described by Sir Francis Nethersole as those who "usually stand stiffest for the country," seemed to find the temper of Commons when they stated that previous funds had been misused and that the King was ill counseled.[75] They saw no actions commensurate to their earlier generosity, but they did see much that was amiss in England. Sir Thomas Edmondes and Sir Richard Weston presented the government's necessities in foreign affairs, but this Parliament was more inclined to look to foreign affairs by looking within England.[76]

1626

The unhappy second Parliament of Charles I was interested in foreign affairs, but its interest was not in the Palatinate. The war against Spain had been fought by sending a naval expedition to Cadiz, but the expedition was a failure which lost money and honor. The Commons, from which many of the opposition leaders of 1625 had been excluded, found a new leader in Sir John Eliot, who pressed the House to inquire into the cause of the Cadiz disaster before it considered any further supply for the war. A committee was established, and its investigations led it to name the Duke of Buckingham as the source of the ills of England at home and abroad. The House of Lords, meanwhile, was devoting itself to the charges of Buckingham against the Earl of Bristol and to Bristol's charges against Buckingham about the negotiations over the Spanish marriage. The crisis of this Parliament came when Commons carried up to the Lords an impeachment of the royal favorite. The King, to save the Duke, dissolved the Parliament.[77]

75. *CSPD, Charles I,* I, 82.

76. *Debates in the House of Commons in 1625,* 77–89; Eliot, *Negotium Posterorum,* II, 24–27, 32–33.

77. Gardiner, VI, 37–121 *passim.*

D'Ewes, a Puritan who never lost his interest in the cause of religion abroad, when writing on the dissolution of the Parliament of 1626, expressed his disappointment that "all those proceedings received a sudden check and stop by this heavy and fatal dissolution; which happened not only most unseasonably in respect of the many blessings we missed at home by it, but also because the King had at this time many great and noble designs abroad for the restoring of God's oppressed Church and Gospel in foreign parts. All men that truly loved God, their King and country had just cause to lament so dismal and sad an accident." [78] For the Parliament, however, foreign affairs were not to be considered until the internal grievances of England were reformed. More and more the trend of parliamentary action was towards a kind of national introspection in which there was less and less to be done in foreign affairs generally and nothing at all for the Palatinate specifically.

1628–1629

The two sessions of the Parliament that began in 1628 contained in them much of the future and some of the past. For the future, this Parliament numbered in its opposition many of the members who would return to Westminster in 1640 to begin to settle what had begun in 1628.[79] From the past, in which a decade of war in Europe had left its marks on England's politics, one problem was ended by action, another by inaction.

The most urgent problem was still the Duke of Buckingham. Sir John Eliot reviewed for the Commons the past mistakes in foreign affairs, and he again placed the blame for

78. D'Ewes, I, 301.

79. William M. Mitchell, *The Rise of the Revolutionary Party in the English House of Commons, 1603–1629* (New York, 1957), 122.

those mistakes upon Buckingham. Two days later (5 June), after Charles had sent a message telling it he would not suffer his ministers to be attacked, the Commons intensified the attack. The Duke was guilty in the eyes of Sir Edward Coke, who said, "And I think the Duke of Buckingham is the cause of all this, and so long as those courses are God will not go with us neither by land or sea . . ." And he was a traitor whom Mr. Valentine denounced: "He which is called the General of soldiers minded to cut our throats: he is the common enemy of the kingdom, and is and must and shall be and can be no other." Although Parliament was prorogued before it could perform its intention and punish the favorite, the same result was accomplished when Felton assassinated the Duke of Buckingham.[80] To many in Parliament and throughout England the Duke had been one way to explain the failures of English diplomacy, money, or arms to secure any good for the Palatinate. Now he was dead; now that explanation was no longer available.

In the condition of religion in England the Puritans saw another explanation for English failures. At a public fast in April 1628, the Commons heard the eminent Puritan divine, Jeremiah Dyke, preach on God's warning to Noah to build the ark. Dyke told his audience that "God gives warning by his graduall departure from a Nation and a Church," and the sure signs of that departure were the entrance of idolatry, the corruption of the ministry, and the failing of a nation's strength. The growth of Arminianism and popery was specific demonstration of God's departure from England, and the troubling of the Church in Europe was a premonition

---

80. Gardiner, VI, 299–325; Lowther, *Notes in Parliament, 1628,* in Historical Manuscript Commission, Thirteenth Report, Appendix, Part VII: *The Manuscripts of the Earl of Lonsdale at Lowther Castle* (London, 1893), 36–37; Edward Hyde, Earl of Clarendon, *The History of the Rebellion and Civil Wars in England,* ed. W. D. Macray (6 vols.; Oxford, 1888), I, 33–34.

of the divine wrath that would come against an unreformed England.[81]

Parliament accepted the sermon's theme and added to it. Sir John Eliot observed England failing and its enemies prevailing as an effect of the toleration of popery.[82] Furthermore, in 1629 the claim was made that popery and its handmaiden, Arminianism within the Church of England, constituted a violation of rights which must have precedence even over violations of the Petition of Right. Mr. Rouse demanded, "This right, in the name of this Nation, I this day claim, and desire that there may be a deep and serious consideration of the violations of it." He was followed by Sir Francis Seymour, who added: "If Religion be not a rule to all our actions what policy can we have? If God fight not our battles, the help of man is in vain. In our defects, the cause thereof is our defect in Religion, and the sins of idolatry and popery." God would not fight for England to redeem the Palatinate because England was defective in religion; for England to regain God's favor, the Parliament must root out idolatry. As a beginning, Phelips proposed "that we may humble ourselves before God by fasting and prayer, that we may bring him again into England into our actions, to go before our armies, that God may crown our actions and bless our counsels." [83] To this request for a fast King Charles replied "that for our protestant friends abroad, fighting would do more good than fasting." [84]

Although the zeal of this Parliament for the cause of true religion was lauded by the Puritans and the dissolution la-

81. Jeremiah Dyke, *A Sermon Preached at the Publicke Fast. To The Commons House of Parliament* (London, 1628), 17–25, 43–47.

82. Eliot, *Negotium Posterorum*, I, 169.

83. *Commons Debates for 1629*, ed. Wallace Notestein and Frances Helen Relf (Minneapolis, 1921), 12–21, 64–72, 95–101.

84. Bulstrode Whitelock, *Memorials of the English Affairs* (4 vols.; Oxford, 1853), I, 33.

mented by them, the temporal cause of the religious brethren in Germany received less attention than in either 1625 or 1626.[85] When in 1621 and 1624 there had been some reason to have hope for the Palatinate, the Puritans had founded their hope in Parliament, where their influence was significant. But conflicts with James and the vision of a cheap, effective war against Spain destroyed the opportunities for direct action; and when in the reign of Charles the Parliament considered foreign affairs at all, the purpose of the consideration was to blame and punish those — Buckingham, the Catholics, the Arminians — whom the Parliament held responsible for the failures. With a fervor that increased from 1625 to 1626 to 1629, Parliament turned to look within England and away from the Palatinate where England had failed.

The Legend of Elizabeth of Bohemia

In spite of enthusiasm (enthusiasm that was frustrated by either inaction or miscarried action) for the Palatinate and all that the Palatinate meant in terms of Calvinism in Germany, by the end of the 1620's it was clear that nothing would, or probably could, be done for the Palatinate by England. Still, not all of the force of enthusiasm was frustrated by failure; some was channeled into a heroine-worship which had begun before the Palatinate was overrun and which endured and grew through the times of lost hopes.

Some part of the vividness of the legend of Elizabeth of Bohemia must be attributed to the manner in which her story was compared with that of Queen Elizabeth. The memory of England's great Elizabeth was becoming a source of near idolatry. Her triumphs over Catholicism and Spain were

85. D'Ewes, I, 399–400; *CSPD, Charles I*, III, 516–517; PRO SP 16/142/94; PRO SP 16/177/8.

turned into the glories of a cult, which might serve as a kind of Protestant Mariology.[86] Elizabeth of Bohemia was also a female champion of the true religion, a woman plotted against by the Catholics, and a ruler attacked by Spain. The difference, of course, was that where Queen Elizabeth had been victorious, Elizabeth of Bohemia, after her moment in Prague, had been driven from place to place until she came to eat an exile's bread in the United Provinces. And it was this defeated "second Queene Elizabeth" to whom the pamphleteers called attention, so that patriotic Protestant Englishmen beheld their beloved Queen — in her namesake — scorned and reviled by her enemies, who were also their enemies.[87]

Elizabeth of Bohemia represented more than just a contrast between England's victorious past and England's defeated present. She represented a possible future, for until 1630 she and her children were the immediate line of succession to the throne of Great Britain. The point was not missed by some extremist individuals in England. In 1623 two justices in Bedfordshire were concerned about a paper in which it was prophesied that a change in religion in that year would be cured only "by one of the name of the maiden Queen," and in 1626 "a man of mean quality" was imprisoned for suggesting that the times would be remedied were Buckingham and Charles killed and Elizabeth of Bohemia sent for.[88] The attraction of the Puritans to the Electoral family was noticed by Archbishop Laud, who had been denounced from the pulpit by the Puritan Henry Burton for deleting from the prayers the usual "mention of the Lady Elizabeth and her children." Laud countered that although he honored Elizabeth he, unlike Prynne, Burton, and Bastwick, did not know how to depart from his allegiance. No matter how pleasing an al-

86. See chap. iii for a discussion of the legend of Queen Elizabeth.
87. Scott, *Second Part of Vox Populi*, 59; Barnes, *Vox Belli*, 37.
88. PRO SP 14/143/87, SP 16/39/35.

ternative the undoubted Protestant Queen of Bohemia might be, a charge of disloyalty to King Charles had to be answered at this time. This reply to Laud was therefore printed: "Prayers might have been continued by his Gr: for the Queene of Bohemia and her Children, without departing from his allegeance, and mens desire of continuance of that prayer, or being offended at the leaving out of it, is not a sufficient reason for his Gr: to inferre a conclusion to charge them with the crime of departing from their allegeance, or for his Gr. suspition of it." [89] The Archbishop had touched the Puritans on a tender spot.[90]

Elizabeth of Bohemia was martyr and perhaps future monarch, but her great appeal in England was as the popular Protestant. Floyd, to his sorrow, learned of her popularity when the Parliament of 1621 came to her defense — a defense which can be summarized here in the words of Sir Dudley Digges: "The noble Lady's worth is such as that the strangers abroade doe honor her and her parents for it. Lett him be whipt through the streetes and that to testyfye to all the world our affection to her and hers, and this to signify to the Lords that theay may have part of this honor." [91] Her popularity had its practical side. Whereas James and Charles usually had great difficulty in raising money from their subjects, as late as 1633 Sir Francis Nethersole in two days obtained backing

89. PRO SP 16/335/69; Henry Burton, *For God, and the King* (n. p., 1636), 143. The quotation is from *Divine and Politike Observations . . . Upon Some Lines in the speech of the Ar. B. of Canterbury, pronounced in the Starre-Chamber upon 14. June, 1637* (Amsterdam, 1638), 33.

90. Birch, *Charles I.* Two interesting sidelights on the popularity of Elizabeth of Bohemia and her family are to be found in this collection: on the scaffold Felton prayed for the King and Queen of Bohemia before he prayed for the Queen of England (I, 442); there is a lamentation on the death of the young Prince of Bohemia, upon whom the "hopes of all the afflicted party were already fixed" (II, 8).

91. *Commons Debates 1621*, III, 123. See also the account of Floyd's case given above in this chapter.

from the London merchants, "a wise and cautious generation in matters of money," for a campaign to raise £31,000 in contributions for Elizabeth. Secretary Windebank in a letter to the King remarked that "this shows there is blood enough in the King's subjects, if the right vein be opened." [92] Hearts also remained open to the unfortunate Elizabeth, and throughout the 1630's there were writers who sustained that loyalty by dedications, by praises of her virtues, and by recitations of her sufferings for the Reformed religion.[93] Although one could do little to aid the professors of religion abroad and although in England too one saw religion tottering, one could, by a firm loyalty to Elizabeth of Bohemia, display a loyalty to her cause — the cause of true religion.

The Palatinate Becomes a Shibboleth

As Elizabeth of Bohemia, in the form of a legendary heroine, survived the ruin of the Palatinate, so too the Palatinate as a symbol survived the Palatinate as a political fact. Gardiner wrote of a decline in English interest in Germany after 1629, and he viewed that decline as the product of public diversion through greater interest in domestic affairs and a diminution in the danger from the continent.[94] Gardiner's view seems partially correct. There were occasional alarms in England, but England was never endangered and became involved actively only by choice — a choice not taken often enough by the government to satisfy Puritan demands. An intensification of interest in domestic affairs did occur, and that shift

92. *CSPD, Charles I*, VI, 90.

93. *Ibid.*, VI, 345–346; [W. Watt], *The Swedish Intelligencer* (London, 1632), "The Fourth Part," 170–174; Vincent Theol., *The Lamentations of Germany* (London, 1638), fifth page of "Preface Exhortatory"; John Vicars, *Englands Hallelu-jah; or, Great Britaines retribution* (London, 1631), stanza 52.

94. Gardiner, VI, 373–376.

was visible before the Parliament of 1628. Nevertheless, there was an enduring core of interest in the Palatinate, but that ongoing interest was concentrated mainly on a symbolic Palatinate rather than the territorial Palatinate.[95]

The Palatinate came to be a figure in sermon imagery, for the events in Germany were a source of ready examples for the English preacher. The banishment of the Reformed ministers before the capture of Heidelberg was used by John Cotton and William Gouge as an example of the departure of the righteous remnant preceding inevitable destruction.[96] Two more members of the Puritan brotherhood, Jeremiah Dyke and Thomas Taylor, treated the Palatinate's destruction as God's forewarning of England.[97] In 1638 a pair of tracts emphasized that the Palatinate was a warning to sinful England to repent of its sins so as to avoid the wrath which had produced the well-known horrors in Germany.[98] As late as 1640 William Bridge told his auditors, English soldiers serving under the Prince of Orange, the reason the Palatinate had been lost: "When we consider the afflictions of Germany, we are ready to say, if such a King or country had stepped in, all this evill had been prevented, the Palatinate restored, and peace setled, but may we not rather say, if our prayers had stepped in, This word telleth us, that our prayers do awaken God, and when God is awakened, then the enemies are destroyed, we see then in truth where the fault lyeth, our pray-

95. See Birch, *Charles I*, II, 280. This is a letter which shows an interest in the political Palatinate as late as 1637.

96. John Cotton, *Gods Promise To His Plantation* (London, 1630), 10; William Gouge, *Gods Three Arrowes: Plague, Famine, Sword, In three Treatises* (London, 1631), 26–27.

97. Dyke, *A Sermon Preached at the Publicke Fast*, 23; Thomas Taylor, *Christs Victorie over the Dragon* (London, 1633), 308.

98. Vincent Theol., *The Lamentations of Germany*, "To the Reader"; L. Br[inckmair], *The Warnings of Germany by Wonderfvll Signes, and strange Prodigies . . . betweene the Yeare 1618 and 1638 Together with a brief relation of the miserable Events which ensued* (London, 1638), 21–22.

ers have not come in full enough, wherefore the lesse we have prayed before, the more let us pray now . . ." [99] These usages of the Palatinate were not of a country invaded by Austria, Spain, and Bavaria; this was a Palatinate which resembled Israel delivered up to Assyria. The Palatinate, like a reference to biblical history, was abstracted out of history to serve as an example and warning to the sinful and forgetful generation in England.

The Palatinate served another function as a symbol: by one's attitude toward the Palatinate one's devotion to the true religion was revealed.[100] Here was a religious test that was meant to separate the true from the false. Lucy Hutchinson, when she looked back upon the foreign policy of King Charles, found him and his policy wanting; for he had betrayed the Protestants abroad because he had looked upon them as Puritans.[101] Charles failed the test; and Archbishop Laud failed a similar, but more exact, test when it was asserted that Laud had struck from a patent "for a collection for the distressed Churches of the Palatinate, the words bearing them to be of the same Religion, which our Church professeth." This writer against Laud reasoned that such a deletion "argueth that he hateth the Religious professors both in that Country where the Queene of Bohemia was borne, and in that wherein shee was maried . . . as a Prelate which either hateth the Queene of Bohemias Religion, or professeth another Religion then shee and her Children doe." [102] Loyalty to the true

99. William Bridge, *The true Souldiers Convoy* (Rotterdam, 1640), 68–69.

100. In a diary entry for 1629 John Rous, a minister, recorded that he asked the news of a fellow minister, who replied: "What newes? Every man askes what newes? Everyman's religion is knowne by his newes; the Puritan talks of Bethlehem Gabor, etc." John Rous, *Diary,* ed. M. A. E. Green, Camden Society, LXVI (London, 1856), 44.

101. Lucy Hutchinson, *Memoirs of the Life of Colonel Hutchinson,* ed. Julius Hutchinson, revised by C. H. Firth (2 vols.; London, 1885), I, 122.

102. *Divine and Politike Observations,* 32–33.

religion could be tested by a shibboleth, and the Palatinate was that shibboleth.

But attitudes toward the Palatinate were more than a determination of religious belief; patriotism, too, could be determined in this manner. The measurement of patriotism against the standard of the Palatinate appeared early. Papists, it was claimed, showed their disaffection to England by their joy at the loss of the Palatinate. The formalist Protestants, by their feeble attitude toward the Palatinate and by their willingness to pander to Spain, showed themselves to be "no true subject" but persons deserving of "an English and a Spanish pension." [103] In contradistinction to disloyal and nominally loyal Englishmen stood the Puritans. The Puritans pointed to themselves as the true subjects who demonstrated their loyalty to England by their support for the Palatinate.[104] They alone passed their own test of patriotism. Apparently, this shibboleth retained some force as late as 1640. In that year a Covenanter pamphlet addressed to England made the point that "all the good Subjects of England" would not come against Scotland; instead, they should join with the Scots to fight for the inheritance of the Electoral family.[105] Even at that late date, the good subject could be called forth and identified by his response to the shibboleth of the Palatinate.

For the English Puritan the symbolic Palatinate survived as a mark of his identification with the true religion and as a sign that he was the true Englishman. Initially, the real Palatinate had captured the interest and enthusiasms of the Puritan because he had regarded it as allied to him by bonds of religion and dynasty. When defeat came, the religion was

103. Scott, *The Interpreter*, 14.

104. PRO SP 14/159/28; Scott, *The Interpreter*, 3, 7; Scott, *Vox Regis*, 21–22.

105. *An Information From The States Of the Kingdome of Scotland, to the Kingdome of England* (Amsterdam, 1640), 6–7.

persecuted, and the Electoral family was exiled. England failed to prevent that defeat, and after the defeat England was incapable of effecting any restoration in Germany. In spite of the zeal of the Puritan for the Palatinate, nothing substantial was done for it. The Palatinate as symbol rather than political fact, however, did provide something for the English Puritan: as a badge of religion and patriotism the Palatinate separated the Puritan from the false and the weak and united him with other godly brethren who were true and strong.

III

Spain

Legends of the Living Past

Spain was the enemy. Spain was the only nation about which the Puritan had a completely clear view. Even in the case of the Palatinate, Christ's Sheep, the Puritan sometimes conceded some cloudiness of view; but in the case of Spain, the Romish Wolf, the Puritan saw with perfect clarity the antagonist — the Antichrist.[1] Spain was all the Puritan most hated. Where other Englishmen usually disliked Spain, the Puritan always hated it; when others sometimes failed to remember their dislike of Spain, the Puritan never forgot his hatred. He did not forget, and he sought to keep alive an English hatred of Spain. This generation of Englishmen were made to see what Spain would do now and in the future by showing them what Spain had done in the past. Englishmen were made to see what they must do to counter Spain by be-

1. The legal questions about the Bohemian Crown and the interpretation that the Palatinate's destruction was caused by sins were two problems which slightly blurred the Puritan view of the Palatinate. See chap. ii.

ing shown what the last generation had done to defeat Spain.

The reign of Queen Elizabeth had had its dangers, but to the Puritan of the early seventeenth century the Elizabethans appeared to have had only victories under the great Queen. Plots had been laid against her and had been foiled; attacks had been mounted against England and had been defeated. Her triumphs were recited and her courage and wisdom praised, for she had seen the Spanish enemy and with divine aid had crushed Spain.[2] The literature in praise of Elizabeth is enormous, but it can be epitomized in the following rude verses written by a preacher:

> Witnesse, o ever witnesse, may those dayes,
> Those Halycon-Dayes of sweet Eliza's Raigne;
> Eliza, worthy Englands endlesse praise,
> That Friend to Faith, That Scourge to Rome, & Spaine:
> All present, past, and future Ages Glorie,
> Worthy prime Place and Grace in datelesse Storie.
> By whom, the Lord so many wonders wrought,
> To whom the Lord so great deliverance gave;
> For whom in their owne Snares hir Foes he caught,
> In whom his Church (poore Church) he oft did save:
> By wondrous, glorious, world-admired protection,
> Such was to Hir and Hirs, Heavens firme affection.[3]

But another Puritan, Thomas Alured, writing to Buckingham in 1620, penned the religious superlative of idolatry for Elizabeth when he called her "that happiest instrument of god, of her sexe since the most blessed virgin marie . . ."[4] Other Elizabethan heroes were reminders to Englishmen that

2. Hutchinson, *Memoirs,* I, 109; Scott, *Essex His Ghost,* "Post Script." Gouge, *Gods Three Arrowes,* 353–361 (this treatise, entitled *Famine,* was dedicated to the Earl and Countess of Warwick).

3. Vicars, *Englands Hallelu-jah,* stanzas 13–14.

4. PRO SP 14/115/67.

great men had fought under Elizabeth for England and against Spain. From among the many heroes Essex and Raleigh were most prominently mentioned by the Puritans. Lucy Hutchinson praised Essex's courage, and she explained that he had been executed by Elizabeth because he had been plotted against by the dissembling James. Thomas Scott, presumably certain of Essex's popularity and orthodoxy, employed the Earl's ghost to remind England of past victories over Spain and to urge England to new efforts against Spain.[5] Raleigh was more immediately remembered; for he not only had been the last of the Elizabethans, but he apparently had been sacrificed by James in order to satisfy Spanish demands. In what was probably his last pamphlet, Scott used "Sir Walter Rawleighs Ghost" to be "Englands Forewarner" against Spanish trickery, and two years later another Puritan writer resorted to the same device to expose Spain's deceits.[6]

Essex and Raleigh were cited as the preeminent examples of warriors against Spain, but a host of other Elizabethan heroes were mentioned. They often were named in roster form, a roll call of heroes who had fought Spain: Cumberland, Drake, the Norrisses, the Veres, Sydney, Willoughby, Gray, Gilbert, Hawkins, Frobisher, Cavendish, Grenville, and Leicester, Burleigh, and Cecil.[7] And when those names were invoked to recall England to emulate their deeds against Spain, this question was asked:

> Where are those spirits that in a Woman's raign
> Sacked Cales & with terror strok all Spain?

5. Hutchinson, *Memoirs*, I, 109; Scott, *Essex His Ghost*, 12–16.

6. Chamberlain, *Letters*, 178; [Thomas Scott], *Sir Walter Rawleighs Ghost, or Englands Forewarner. Discovering a secret Consultation, newly holden in the Court of Spaine* (Utrecht, 1626), *passim;* J. R., *The Spy,* sig. D2; PRO SP 14/118/104.

7. *Gallants, to Bohemia, Or let us to the Warres again* (London, ca. 1632), in *Pepys Ballads*, photostats 102–103; J. R., *The Spy,* sig. A1v, D2; Scott, *Vox Coeli,* 34–37.

Harrowed their Indian fleet, drowned their men
And made their twelve Apostles less by tenn? [8]

Elizabeth and her galaxy of heroes were legendary because
of their victories over Spain; and, of course, their greatest
deed was the defeat of the Spanish Armada. The year '88 was
immortal. The Armada had been a grave danger, but Protestant England had openly met and defeated Catholic Spain.
The Puritans still wanted it that way, for God had been with
England when England had fought Spain:

This was the Lord; Let thankefull hearts declare it,
For, tis exceeding wondrous in our Eares;
That yeere of Eighty-Eight, o never spare it,
To blaze the praise of That yeere, all thy yeeres:
Let English Isre'll, sing and say all wayes,
Not unto us, but to the Lord be prayse.[9]

The '88 represented a deed done cleanly, without compromis-
ings and jugglings; it illustrated the way in which the Elizabethans had made England glorious. The '88 also reminded
England that the Spaniard was yet its foe, for some in England feared that the English had changed so much since the
days of the Armada that no longer could they confidently
face Spain. The legends of the living past reminded the English that their Elizabethan heroes were gone but that their
enemy remained.[10]

8. PRO SP 14/118/104.
9. Vicars, *Englands Hallelu-jah*, stanza 25.
10. George, *The Protestant Mind of the English Reformation, 1570–1640*,
252–253; Vicars, *Englands Hallelu-jah*, stanzas 19–25; Eliot, *Negotium Posterorum*, I, 76–77; Chamberlain, *Letters*, 350; Edmund Garrard, *The Countrie
Gentleman Moderator* (London, 1624), 48–49, 52–55. Garrard's work favored
alliances between England and Spain. When the author wrote on the Armada,
he blamed the venture on the Pope; and he went on to note that, as Spain
was the loser, England should be willing to forget it. The ill feelings between
the two countries were caused by religious zealots in Spain and England.

The Spanish Enemy

The Puritan saw Spain and the Roman Catholic Church as one inseparable danger. He knew that past conspiracies in England had been plotted by the Papists to further a Spanish end, and he knew the Spanish pursuit of empire furthered the cause of the Romish faith. Hence, Spain and the Catholics acted as one to subvert or conquer England and to convert or destroy religion in England. It followed then that Spanish gains were Catholic victories, and English Catholics were traitors for Spain. This identification of Spain and Catholicism as the same danger was stated by Thomas Scott in *Vox Populi,* the pamphlet which most forcefully brought him to the attention of the English people and the government of James I. Scott dramatized the Puritan attitude to Spain and Catholic by describing a fictitious meeting of the Spanish Council of State. At this meeting Count Gondomar spoke about the Spanish goal of a universal monarchy, and Scott gave Gondomar this speech:

> What the ignorant call treason, if it be on this behalf is truth; & what they call truth, if it be against him is treason: & thus all our peace, our warre, our treaties, mariages, and whatsoever intendement else of ours, aimes at this principall end, to get the whole possession of the world, and to reduce all to unitie under one temporall head, that our King may truly be what he is stiled, the catholick and universal King . . . We see . . . in England especially, where at once they learne to obey the Church of Rome as their mother, to acknowledge the catholique King as their father, and to hate their owne King as an heretique and an usurper. So we see Religion and the State are coupled together, laugh and weep,

flourish and fade, and participate of eithers fortune, as growing upon one stock of policy . . .[11]

Spain and Rome were the same enemy to England inasmuch as they both appeared to the Puritan to be seeking a Catholic Spanish universal monarchy. To the Puritan in the seventeenth century this enemy, following the same pattern employed in the legendary age of Elizabeth, was attacking on two fronts. First, there was the Spanish Empire and its allies attacking with diplomacy and arms: this was the external enemy. Second, the Puritan saw an assault within England by Catholic plots and subversions, which were made to serve Spain. The Puritan saw England attacked from within and without, but both thrusts came from the same enemy — the enemy that Elizabeth had defeated — Spain.[12]

The External Enemy

The Puritans beheld in Spain a military danger to Eng-

11. [Thomas Scott], *Vox Populi or Newes From Spayne* (n. p., 1620), sig. A4. This, the first and most famous of Scott's attacks on Spain, was published four times in 1620. The numerous contemporary references to it indicate that it was the initial cause of public awareness about the proposed Spanish match. See also *The Fortescue Papers,* 143–144; *CSPD, James I,* X, 208; Birch, *Charles I,* I, 122–123. The letter in Birch suggests that Scott was murdered in the Netherlands in 1626 to prevent pamphlet attacks by him against the government of Charles I and the Duke of Buckingham. *Vox Populi* reappeared later in the century under a different title and authorship. See Richard Dugdale, *A Narrative of the Wicked Plots carried on by Seignior Gondamore and Spanish faction* (London, 1679), in *Harleian Miscellany,* ed. W. Oldys (12 vols.; London, 1808–1811), III, 327–341. See also Charles H. Carter, *The Secret Diplomacy of the Hapsburgs, 1598–1625* (New York, 1964), 120–122.

12. One of the most elaborate discourses on the Roman-Hapsburg conspiracy theme is contained in an anonymous manuscript in the Folger Shakespeare Library, MS V.a. 24, ca. 1620, "In what lamentable estate . . ." Every trouble in Europe and England is explained as a part of this universal plot. However, when the author upholds James as the wise dissembler, turning Catholic intrigues into English benefits, the work seems to crumble into contradictions. It is difficult to decide whether this was intended as an apology or a burlesque.

land, a danger which sprang from Spanish ambitions for a universal monarchy. Of course, the Spanish imperialism was a threat against other nations too, and when Scott wrote against Spain he reminded all the Princes of Christendom that they were also objects of Spanish avarice. *The Spaniards Perpetuall Designes To An Universall Monarchie* showed an English public the encirclement of France by the Hapsburgs, and another work told the same audience that Germany was the heart of Europe and that "if Germanie as the heart be possest by the Spaniard, who strives to get dominion over all Europe, the rest of the Princes shall not long draw or enjoy any vitall life or spirits." [13] The clear inference to be drawn by the English reader was that England had to be a part of the Spanish plan; England only waited its turn. In fact, England could be certain of its place in the Spanish grand design; for, as a speaker in the Parliament of 1621 reminded the Commons, a stronger England previously had frustrated Spain's aspiration "to be monarch of the west." [14]

The Puritan was aware that Spain, when its purposes were best served, sometimes masked its ambitions. England had to be made to see through the mask in order to understand where and how Spanish actions, although disguised, were actually and constantly moving in accord with the Spanish program. The Palatinate was a ready example: to rule Europe, Spain had to secure Germany, and to secure Germany,

13. [Thomas Scott], *A Second Part of Spanish Practises* (n. p., 1624), the second of three parts of this unpaginated pamphlet. *The Spaniards Perpetuall Designes To An Universall Monarchie* (London [?], 1624), was asserted by Scott to be a translation from the French, and it reads that way; whether or not it was a translation is unimportant here, for its significance is that Scott offered it to the English public to show them the Spanish danger. The quotation is from [Thomas Scott], *Certaine Reasons and Arguments of Policie, Why the King of England should hereafter give over all further Treatie, and enter into warre with the Spaniard* (n. p., 1624), 10. See also *Tom Tell-Troath*, in *Somers Tracts*, II, 479–480; Ball, *Life of Preston*, 108.

14. *Commons Debates 1621*, II, 208.

Spain had to conquer the strategic stronghold of the Reformed Church. The Palatinate was attacked, and the Church was distressed; but Spain claimed all this was done by Bavaria and the Emperor. The Puritan would have none of this legal fiction, which the pacific James accepted. The Puritan knew that the army which ravaged the Palatinate was a Spanish army commanded by Spinola, the Spanish general. The fact that it was Spain — though thinly disguised — that was operating against the Elector Palatine caused the Commons in 1621 to protest vigorously the sale of English ordnance to Spain, for the members found it strange in the extreme that Englishmen might have to fight against English guns in Spanish hands.[15] By 1624 Spain was named openly as the real enemy. In Parliament and in pamphlet the disguise was torn away for the public to observe Spanish actions matching Spanish designs.[16] Those in England who saw Spain to be the real enemy, the perpetual enemy, also asserted that England must meet the real enemy, not the straw enemies put up by Spanish trickery to deceive England. England had to fight Spain.

England, however, could not war against Spain so long as the King of England treated with Spain. The Puritans were certain that James was being tricked by the Spaniards, and treaties and negotiations about treaties were seen to be another form of Spanish deceit. England was disadvantaged by dealing sincerely with an enemy that dealt falsely; and such false dealings were said to be a tradition of the Hapsburgs, who always had gained from treaties.[17] Since Spain was always false in treaties, it was stressed that England should follow the example of the patriotic Puritan and shun "false

15. *Ibid.*, II, 69–72; Chamberlain, *Letters*, 350; Leighton, *Speculum Belli sacri*, 43–45; *Tom Tell–Troath*, in *Somers Tracts*, II, 477.

16. Winchilsea MS, "1624," fols. 10v–11v; Gurney MS, "1624," 44–46; Scott, *Vox Dei* (n. p., 1624), 4, and *A Speech By Sir Edward Cicell*, 1–2.

17. *Commons Debates 1621*, III, 451–458; Gurney MS, "1624," 44, 54–55.

favours . . . from a true foe." When Spain, "being true to nothing but their owne grounded Maximes," invited England to new treaties, the Puritan denounced the invitation as being "a dishonour they have obtruded upon our Nation and Religion . . ."[18]

Spanish treaties were more than a dishonor to England; in that the treaties weakened England, they were a danger. England was weakened when it negotiated with Spain because the negotiations tended to discourage England's allies. The German Princes could not be rallied to aid the Palatinate against Spain while they saw England and Spain joined in treaty, nor could the Dutch be in any way comforted by the knowledge that England was at peace with their foe.[19] Another way in which England was said to be dangerously weakened by engaging in Spanish treaties was that such treaties lulled the English into a sleep of false security. The false security produced by the treaties unmanned the English, who now were given over to "Stage-Plays, Maskes, Revels and Carowsings" instead of being practiced in martial exercises. The navy even lay rotting at Chatham and Rochester while King James allowed England to become persuaded of false Spain's false treaties.[20]

To regain lost honor, friends, and glory, England, it was urged, had to cease placing any trust in Spain. The treaties had to be broken, negotiations halted. The alternative to treaties had to be taken: "Let us not treat with him, but as I said before with our swords in our hands, his treaties otherwaies are ominous."[21]

The Puritans rejected any accommodation with Spain, for

18. Scott, *The Interpreter*, 3, and *A Second Part of Spanish Practises*, 3.
19. Gurney MS, "1624," 54–55, 58.
20. Scott, *The Belgick Souldier*, 37–45; Scott, *Vox Coeli*, 36–37 (source of quotation).
21. Scott, *A Speech By Sir Edward Cicell*, 5; see also Scott, *The Belgick Souldier*, 42.

Spanish ambitions could not be accommodated without English losses. Spanish ambitions had to be halted with the sword, as they had been halted by Queen Elizabeth. Because the Puritans equated the territorial designs of Spain with the designs of the Roman Church to regain the lost nations, a war against Spain meant a crusade, a holy war against the Romish Spanish infidel. "There is a Moab then in the world, O England, a fit object for thy sword, a meete foe to fight withall." England dared not withhold the sword from the blood of this Moab, or England would be disobedient to God and fall under God's curse. "Oh round them in their eare, present thy selfe to their eyes, that the sight of thee may make them stirre in the Lords quarrell, who have been backward all this while, and make them constant that have begunne, untill they have done the worke of the Lord." [22]

England had to war against Spain or suffer divine wrath; however, when the English fought under divine injunction, they were assured of victory. In *Vox Dei*, which was only one of Scott's many tracts in favor of a Spanish war, the exiled preacher demonstrated that the highest good for man was to fight for the true religion. The example was given of the boy David to whom God gave the strength to slay Goliath and thereby protect the state and the church, which had been scorned and attacked by the heathens.[23] Victory was certain in a war for God's cause; and although individual soldiers would be killed, a soldier slain in a battle for the true religion was taken up by the angels.[24] The self-confidence and self-assurance which marked those who would fight in God's cause were not confined to the Puritans; thus in 1624, when Buckingham, the Parliament, and the Puritans were agreed on war, there was a truly popular enthusiasm for an English

22. Barnes, *Vox Belli*, 33–36 (the quotation is on 33).
23. Scott, *Vox Dei*, 1–18.
24. Gouge, *Gods Three Arrowes*, 248.

crusade.[25] England would obey the commandment and fight for God's Church, and God would fight for England. England was exhorted: "That every one may be ready with the Machabes to defend the Sanctuary of the Lord; And with true English hearts, not onely fight in the defence of their Countrey, but when God commands, not to spare, to goe on and prepare, and let every one prepare himselfe . . . And the God of heaven prepare your hearts, wayes, words, deeds, and dealings, to be vigilant and carefull to provide for us: and we with Gods helpe will be carefull to fight for you. And so the God of heaven Fight for us all." [26]

"Warre hath been better than peace, and that the Commonwealth and Religion of England have had their glory and propagation by opposing Antichrist, and in plaine termes reputing Spain our Antagonist . . ." [27] This proposition that war against the Romish Spanish enemy would prosper England was a reasonable inference from the concept that England's war against Spain was not only a divine command but a covenant on the part of God to fight for England against the enemy of God's Church. Further assurances were offered on this point: the English were shown that when other nations, notably the United Provinces, warred against Spain, they prospered exceedingly great. In the House of Commons Sir John Eliot acknowledged war to be costly, but he went on to remind the House "that the war with Spaine is our Indies that there wee shall fetch wealth and happines . . ." [28] Another source of the certainty of profitable victory over Spain was the belief that Queen Elizabeth had not only found war with Spain to be the course of England's safety, but that

25. Maclear, *Huntington Library Quarterly*, 21 (February 1958), 115; *CSPD, James I*, XI, 291; Sir Philip Warwick, *Memoirs of the Reign of King Charles the First* (Edinburgh, 1813), 4.

26. Scott, *The Belgick Souldier*, 45.

27. *Ibid.*, 2.

28. *Ibid.*, 29–37; Gurney MS, "1624," 105, 125–126 (source of quotation).

she had made her wars profitable to England. Elizabeth's victorious policy was a precedent showing that God prospered a crusading England.[29]

Many in England thought that the best method of fighting Spain was to be found in the Elizabethan example, which had been blessed by success. There was the unshakable opinion that England warred best (also, less expensively) when England's navy did the fighting. On the seas England could give the law to Spain; therefore, England ought to choose that means rather than the more wasteful method of fighting a land war in Europe. This naval war plan had strong advocates in Parliament, where financial considerations carried much weight.[30] In Parliament and out of it plans for a naval war against Spain received detailed attention, and the area was even specified in which it was believed the English navy could most effectively destroy Spanish power. The argument ran that Spain, for all its ambitions, was not fearfully strong in itself; Spain's strength was considerable only as long as New World gold and silver supplied the Spanish treasury. Without that constant supply Spain could not pay the great land armies, which would surely mutiny for want of pay, and thus Spanish power would be destroyed. England, consequently, had to attack Spain's source of strength, which was thought to be easily susceptible to the actions of the English navy. The navy, even if it did not capture or sink the treasure fleets, would pose such a grave threat that Spain would be required to provide prohibitively expensive convoys, which inevitably would beggar Spain and bring about the desired destruction of the enemy.[31]

29. Scott, *Vox Coeli,* 34, 38.

30. *Ibid.,* 36–37; *Commons Debates 1621,* III, 452–453, 461–462; Chamberlain, *Letters,* 412.

31. *Commons Debates 1621,* III, 456–458; Scott, *Vox Dei,* 5; [Thomas Scott], *An Experimentall Discoverie of Spanish Practises or The Counsell of a well-wishing Souldier, for the good of his Prince and State* (London [?], 1623), 50–51.

The prospect of war as the best way to deal with the power and ambition of Spain was, indeed, made attractive. War was seen as the good old English way to remove the external Spanish danger. To war against Moabitish Spain was to do God's will in a way sanctioned by past English triumphs. Also, war against Spain was popular with the nation; in fact, such a war retained its popular appeal long after the real war against Spain had failed unspectacularly.[32]

The Internal Enemy

The English Puritans detested Romanism and Romanists. The Roman Catholic Church was the antithesis of the Calvinist Church, and in Romanism the Puritan beheld the way of the Antichrist. Theology, ceremony, polity, and history were elements of the bitter antagonism; but nothing evoked a more active hatred than the Puritan equation of Catholicism and Spain. This aspect of anti-Romanism sustained a religious definition of patriotism, for it imposed upon the English Catholics not only the burden of a different religious faith but also the damnation of owing a foreign loyalty. If English Catholics, by the fact that they were Catholics, were thought to be part of the internal attack by Spain against England, then they were all dangerous traitors to the nation. They were not Englishmen who were Catholics; they were Spaniards operating within England to subvert England for the imperial designs of the Most Catholic King of Spain.

The Jesuits, the professional spearhead of popery, were

32. PRO SP 16/372/7. Another enduring aspect of the hatred of Spain as an external enemy was the presence of the Spanish in the New World. L. B. Wright, in the chapter entitled "A Western Canaan" in *Religion and Empire* (Chapel Hill, 1943), treats the anti-Catholic and anti-Spanish sentiment which served to encourage an English Protestant counter-empire in the New World. See also *ibid.*, 155–156, and Scott, *An Experimentall Discoverie of Spanish Practises*, 34–45.

held to be the organizers and commanders for Spain of the English Catholics. Pamphleteers explained how the depraved and treacherous Jesuits had stirred up confusions in Bohemia, how Spain maintained and trained English Jesuits for operations in England, and, of course, how Gunpowder Plot had been a Jesuit device.[33] Usually the Jesuits worked in secret; but on the occasion of the fatal vespers at Black Friars on 26 October 1623, the Jesuit machinations in England were opened, as if by divine providence, for English eyes to see. The incident was a service attended by Catholics and proselytes and conducted by Jesuits; but when a Jesuit began to preach, the floor of the overcrowded room collapsed, killing the preacher and many of the congregation. The fact that in the Roman calendar the date of the disaster was the anniversary of Gunpowder Plot added great significance to this revelation of Jesuit workings in England, and there was no shortage of writers to note the date and the example in an outpouring of uncharitable and gleeful tracts.[34] Thus, this terrible event was used to demonstrate that the Jesuits were infiltrating England, working among the English Catholics, and seeking converts to treason for Spain.

33. *Troubles in Bohemia and other kingdomes procured by Jesuits* (n. p., 1619); James Wadsworth, *The English Spanish Pilgrime. Or, A New Discoverie of Spanish Popery and Jesuiticall Stratagems. With the estate of the English Pentioners and Fugitives under the King of Spaines Dominions, and elsewhere at this present* (London, 1630); [Thomas Scott], *Digitus Dei* (n. p., 1623), 1–23 *passim; Commons Debates 1621,* III, 453; *Debates in the House of Commons in 1625,* 140–141.

34. *Something Written by occasion of that fatall and memorable accident in the Blacke Friers* (n. p., 1623); W[illiam] C[rashaw], *The Fatall Vesper, or A True and Punctuall Relation of that lamentable and fearefull accident . . . by the fall of a roome in the Black-Friers in which were assembled many people at a Sermon, which was to be preached by Father Drurie a Jesuite* (London, 1623); John Gee, *The Foot out of the Snare* (London, 1624); Scott, *The Second Part of Vox Populi,* 30–32, and *Digitus Dei,* 23; Jeremiah Dyke, *Good Conscience: Or A Treatise Shewing the Nature, Meanes, Marks, Benefit, and Necessity thereof* (London, 1624), 326.

Naturally, the English Catholics were believed to be the best source of Jesuit recruits for their Spanish master. The Puritan regarded the English Catholics as virtual aliens, for he knew them to be dependents of the King of Spain. They were English in residence but Spanish in loyalty. Religion was an insufficient tie to bind some Catholic nations to Spain; but as Christopher Brooke observed in Commons, "only our English papists of all the world affect Spaine . . ."[35] And in 1628 Sir John Eliot asserted that it was "the verie object of their faith . . . to advance the Spa: greatness . . ."[36] Others went so far as to claim that the English Catholics knew no other loyalty than their loyalty to Spain;[37] and this point that a Spanish loyalty was owed by all English Catholics was epitomized in an epigram:

> His Character abridg'd if you will have
> Hee is Spaynes subject and a Romish slave.[38]

Charged with being loyal to Spain, whose designs against the English nation and religion were everywhere denounced, the English Catholics had to be considered traitors to England. Sir Edward Coke, that source of countless precedents and tiresome speeches, recalled that in '88 Philip II had assured the Catholics of England they were dearer to him than his Castilians.[39] And when Parliament urged a Spanish war in 1624, the recusants were denounced as a dangerous Spanish faction, for with the prospect of war the recusants threatened an armed rising that could ease the way for a Spanish invasion. This was the gravest sort of internal menace; for, insofar as their Roman religion required a Spanish loyalty,

35. Gurney MS, "1624," 58.
36. Eliot, *Negotium Posterorum*, I, 169.
37. William Hampton, *A Proclamation of Warre from the Lord of Hosts* (London, 1627), 18–22; Scott, *A Speech By Sir Edward Cicell*, 3.
38. Scott, *The Interpreter*, 16.
39. *Notes in Parliament 1628*, 40.

so their Spanish loyalty required treason against England.[40]

An armed rebellion by the recusants would enhance the success of a Spanish invasion; but even when an invasion was not expected, the recusants were accused of laboring for Spain by weakening England: "With their craft they have undermined our wit, they have undermined our State; and which is worst of all, they have undermined, yea and almost blowen up the power of our religion; they have made Israel naked, and Juda contemptible and bar . . ."[41] The Puritans saw the Catholics gain converts, thereby enfeebling English resistance to Catholicism and Spain. And with a sense of horror they attributed the increased strength of popery to the government's relaxation of the laws against the Catholics. The Puritans feared a toleration which could only strengthen an internal enemy whose real allegiance was to England's foe.[42]

The Jesuits and recusants clearly could be identified with Spanish aggression. Often the Puritan only had to remind the English public of the part played by those Spanish agents and English traitors in the plots against Elizabeth and the Gunpowder Plot in order to demonstrate the danger of the internal enemy. But in the seventeenth century the Puritan claimed to see a new danger—one that had not been present at the time of Elizabeth. Under the ill-defined banner of Arminianism the Puritan saw the hosts of Spain in a new and subtle guise, which nonetheless did not obscure the mark of the beast and the badge of Spain.

Unable easily to conquer England, Spain and Rome were said to have conspired to subvert the English Church by means of the Arminian heresy, which, while appearing as a Protestant foe of Romanism, was actually provoking a fatal

40. Winchilsea MS, "1624," fols. 44v–45, 47–47v; Scott, *Vox Regis*, 21–22; PRO SP 14/142/22, II; *CSPD, Charles I*, I, 75.

41. Leighton, *Speculum Belli sacri*, 153.

42. Eliot, *Negotium Posterorum*, I, 169; *Diary of Walter Yonge*, 58; Scott, *Boanerges*, 20; Jordan, *The Development of Religious Toleration*, II, 97–100.

schism in Protestantism. This subversive heresy appealed to ambitious clergymen and courtiers, who by it rose to places of power from which they could suppress the true religion.[43]

With a fervor that grew more intense with each meeting of Parliament under Charles I, the Puritans condemned the Arminians and the favor shown of them.[44] However, the alleged disloyalty of the Arminians was as fiercely attacked as the heresy of Arminius. The Arminians from their vantage point within England and within the Church of England were destroying religion, liberty, and the nation. They were agents of Spain. In a violent and colorful speech to Commons in 1629, a Puritan, Francis Rouse, made all the connections: "Yea, I desire that we may look into the belly and bowels of this Trojan horse, to see if there be not men in it ready to open the gates to Romish tyranny and Spanish monarchy. For an Arminian is the spawn of a Papist; and if there come the warmth of favour upon him, you shall see him turn into one of those frogs that rise out of the bottomless pit. And if you mark it well, you shall see an Arminian reaching out his hand to a Papist, a Papist to a Jesuit, a Jesuit gives one hand to the Pope and other to the King of Spain . . ." [45] Alexander Leighton in one of his long and violent polemics appealed to this Parliament to beware of "the Arminianized, or right down Popish Prelate, the bellie-serving Machiavell, the state-betraying Papist" who "by home-bred sedition and disorder of Church & State" would cheaply deliver England to Spain.[46] Theological and ceremonial disagreement with stern Protestantism was not simply disagreement, it was heresy. And

43. J. R., *The Spy,* sig. C1–C1v; Scott, *Boanerges,* 3, 25; PRO SP 16/335/69; Alexander Leighton, *An Appeal to the Parliament; Or Sions Plea against the Prelacie* (Amsterdam [?], 1628), 120, 234–235, 260.

44. *Notes in Parliament 1628,* 36–43; *Commons Debates 1629,* 12–21, 64–72, 95–101.

45. *Commons Debates 1629,* 13; for Rouse, see *DNB.*

46. Leighton, *An Appeal to the Parliament,* 179.

heretics were not only guilty of religious error, they were guilty of treason. They were the Trojan horse of Spanish imperialism.[47]

Jesuit agents, English Catholic traitors, and Arminian subversives composed the Spanish attack from within England. The Puritans, seeing the danger, knew it must be met or England and the true religion in England would fall to Romish Spain. Proposals on how to defeat the external Spanish enemy relied upon Elizabethan precedents, and the proposals that were offered to eliminate the internal Spanish enemy usually followed the same pattern.

The Jesuit danger could be limited whenever the government began to enforce the already existing laws against the Jesuits. For these servants of the Spanish master there was banishment or imprisonment. When in 1624 King James agreed to a stricter enforcement of the laws, Thomas Scott hailed the change with the exultant prayer, "O blessed by God for this alteration." [48] But enforcement did not remain constant, and later Parliaments petitioned that the Jesuits be rendered harmless in order that England might enjoy internal safety.[49]

The English Catholics could not all be banished or imprisoned, but some proposed courses could lessen the danger of their threat. They could rise in armed rebellion; therefore they must be disarmed. For the safety of England they could not be allowed to increase in numbers; therefore, toleration of them by means of relaxation of the laws must cease, and the Catholic religious services must be suppressed totally.

47. Jordan, *The Development of Religious Toleration*, II, 117–129; Godfrey Davies, "Arminian versus Puritan in England, ca. 1620–1640," *The Huntington Library Bulletin*, No. 5 (April 1934), 163–164.

48. [Thomas Scott], *Englands Joy, For Suppressing the Papists, and banishing the Priests and Jesuites* (n. p., 1624), 2.

49. *Debates in the House of Commons in 1625*, 20–21, 140–141; Leighton, *Speculum Belli sacri*, 154, 307–308.

Denied priests and services, English Catholicism, it was believed, would wither; and that decline could be further hastened by the imposition of financial penalties and the proper religious education of the children of recusants.[50] In 1624 Sir John Eliot neatly tied together the problem and the solution when he advocated that the war against Spain be financed with heavy taxes on the English Catholics.[51] By such means the potential rebels and certain traitors could be made less dangerous to England's security, while Spain would lose its largest faction of adherents within England.

The Arminians, charged with undermining England from within its institutions of church and government, had to be rooted out of their places. Parliament exercised itself by investigating, naming, and denouncing Arminians; and several appeals for reform were presented to Charles.[52] One writer, in urging Charles to purge church and court of these traitors, warned the King that the Arminians were a danger to his crown.[53] Although the Arminians were in no way purged at the time of the dissolution of the Parliament of 1629, they did become a danger to the King, who had not removed them, when the Parliament of 1640 began to reform the Church of England root and branch.

The Infanta of Spain

The Spanish match was more than a great example of Spanish policies towards England; it was the focus of Puritan

50. Scott, *Digitus Dei,* 14; Winchilsea MS, "1624," fol. 47–47v; *Commons Debates 1621,* III, 461–462; *Debates in the House of Lords 1624 and 1626,* 53–57; *Debates in the House of Commons in 1625,* 18–20.

51. Gurney MS, "1624," 46.

52. *Notes in Parliament 1628,* 39–40; *Commons Debates 1629,* 17–21, 24–28, 64–72, 95–101; [Sir Robert Bruce Cotton], *The Danger wherein the Kingdome now standeth, & the Remedie* (n. p., 1628), 12.

53. J. R., *The Spy,* sigs. E3v–E4v, F4v–G1.

fears about Spain's external and internal threat to England. So large and fearful loomed the marriage with the Infanta that an English public opinion was aroused; and the zeal that informed and stirred the public against the Spanish match was mainly the zeal of the English Puritans, who on this issue led and captured a fearful public.[54]

Preachers warned their congregations of the perils to religion and nation from a marriage with a Romish Spanish Princess, while Scripture and history were cited to remind the auditors of the necessary results of matches with idolaters and especially with Spanish idolators.[55] Neither a royal proclamation nor diocesan discipline silenced this pulpit outcry.[56] When preachers were punished for their explications, they would turn to implications. The denunciation by implication produced its intended effect on a congregation. D'Ewes recorded an example: "On Sunday, the 25th day of this month, preached one Mr. Claydon, (minister of Hackney, near London,) at St. Paul's Cross; and cited a story out of our Chronicles, of a Spanish sheep, brought into England in Edward the First's time, which infected most of the sheep of England with a murrain, and prayed God no more such sheep might be brought over from thence hither; at which many of his hearers cried out 'Amen.' " [57]

Pamphleteers also addressed the public on the Spanish attack that appeared as a royal bride. The power of the government was brought to bear upon the press, but the pamphlets

54. Scott, *Vox Coeli,* third page of dedication to Parliament; he named Alured, Whiting, Everard, Clayton, Ward, and himself for having written or preached against the Spanish match. At the request of a peer, John Preston, according to his contemporary biographer, wrote anonymously against the marriage. Ball, *Life of Preston,* 59–60.

55. PRO SP 14/123/105; Birch, *James I,* II, 265–266; Chamberlain, *Letters,* 486.

56. *CSPD, James I,* X, 201; Birch, *James I,* II, 329–330, 392.

57. D'Ewes, I, 219–220.

continued to be published by secret presses and continental presses.[58] An English public heard and read these fierce criticisms of the Spanish match; and violent reactions, even threatening the King's life, were the responses of some.[59] But the Puritan preachers evoked a larger response from the English public, which now was aroused to the Spanish danger; and this public concern focused on the Infanta of Spain.[60]

The very negotiations for a marriage with Spain were, it was claimed, a part of Spain's conquest plans. Scott warned that negotiations were a piece of Spanish trickery; for while Spain dangled the prospect of the marriage before James, Spanish armies overran the Palatinate, attacked the Netherlands, and everywhere endangered the professors of true religion. As long as Spanish treaties enchanted England's King, Spain need have no fear of effective English interference with its territorial aggrandizement. Thus, even if Spanish intentions for the marriage treaty were insincere, Spain was gaining time and territory from the negotiations in which it had ensnared James. Of course, when Spain gained at the expense of England's true friends and coreligionists, England was endangered.[61]

False treaties were a danger, but the Puritans expressed real horror at the fate of England were the Infanta actually to become Princess of Wales. England, married to Spain, would have to desert its allies, especially the United Provinces. The distressed in Germany would have no hope of

58. *Ibid.*, I, 158–159; *CSPD, James I*, X, 281; L. B. Wright, "Propaganda against James I's 'Appeasement' of Spain," *Huntington Library Quarterly*, 6 (February 1943), 171.

59. *CSPD, James I*, X, 351; Birch, *James I*, II, 233.

60. *Harley Letters and Papers*, 17; Davies, *Huntington Library Quarterly*, 3 (October 1939), 9.

61. Scott, *Vox Populi*, sig. B1v–B2, *The Second Part of Vox Populi*, 59, and *A Second Part of Spanish Practises*, 1–3.

succour; the welfare of all Christendom would be threatened. These were said to be the probable consequences of England's being joined to Spain by a dynastic alliance.[62]

An England bereft of allies would be seriously endangered, but the Puritans also envisioned the worst of all possible events: the Spanish match could mean Spanish invasion. To some this total disaster was more than a fearful possibility; Scott wrote that when Prince Charles had been in Spain, the Spaniards had advised him to exterminate the Protestants in England with the aid of the Spanish army.[63] What images this announcement evoked in English minds can only be imagined; but the Marian persecutions, Antwerp, and, more recently, Bohemia and the Palatinate were vivid memories and present realities. In 1631, the year of the sack of Magdeburg, another preacher-polemicist recalled England's deliverance from the Infanta of Spain and her brother's forces:

> Some Trojan-Horse, by Spaines Pelasgan Art,
> With sacred shew, our Kingdome might have entred;
> A Spanish Fleet (at least) t'uphold the part,
> Of urged Reformation had bin ventred:
>   A Fleet (I say) full fraught with arm'd protection,
>   To bring the Puritans to due subjection.[64]

The external threat to England from the Spanish match was made very real indeed.

The Infanta of Spain was also the focus of Puritan fears about the Spanish attack from within England, and in pamphlet and sermon these fears were communicated to the wider English audience. The Spanish match, it was believed, would encourage and prosper the cause of the English Catholics and weaken or destroy the cause of true religion in England.

62. Vicars, *Englands Hallelu-jah*, stanza 52; D'Ewes, I, 158–159; Scott, *Boanerges*, 32.

63. Scott, *Vox Coeli*, fourth page of dedication to Parliament.

64. Vicars, *Englands Hallelu-jah*, stanza 49.

The Infanta in England would raise a Spanish faction at court, for the courtiers would find wealth and favor to be in her gift. A Romish fashion would be the entrance to court, and from that center of power it would spread outward and infect the whole kingdom. Thomas Alured, a noted Puritan minister, admonished Buckingham in a long letter not to permit his high position, which was likened to Joseph's, to be used for so ungodly a purpose, but the courtiers seem to have treated with contempt the charge that by supporting the marriage they were abetting an enemy.[65] Those Englishmen who already were Catholics and therefore friends to Spain would by the terms of the match enjoy a greater toleration from the government, and toleration heartened and assisted them. This peril was debated in a fictional confrontation between Queen Elizabeth, the symbol of the Protestant English, and Queen Mary, the symbol of the pro-Spanish Catholic English.

> Q. E. This would be musicke indeede for the Romane Catholiques of England, if it should take effect; for the very first newes thereof, made them flap their wings, as if they were ready to crowe.

> Q. M. Yea, for they hope, and which is more, they know, that if it prove a Match, That the Infanta will soone introduced the Masse, and Usher in the Pope; therefore they have reason to rejoyce at it.[66]

In particular, one remonstrance against the toleration of popery which would follow the marriage gave the government exceptional concern. The cause of the concern was a published letter to James from Archbishop Abbot, no favorer of Rome, in which denunciation and malediction were heaped upon the match and any toleration of the recusants. The letter was a

65. PRO SP 14/115/67; Scott, *Vox Populi,* sig. B1v–B2.
66. Scott, *Vox Coeli,* 39.

forgery; but an alarmed correspondence between Secretary Calvert and Secretary Conway told of the letter's wide circulation, harmful effects, and, interestingly, the correspondents' belief that so many different persons might have issued the forgery that it "would be an endless, fruitless, and expensive task" to find the real author.[67]

A strengthening of the English Catholics by means of the Spanish match had to imply the weakening of English Protestantism. As the Infanta's religion would be the opening for Catholicism among the courtiers, so too would Roman temptations sway some members of the Anglican clergy. A clergyman darkly wrote of his fears on that point: "That which is sometimes muttered, or spoken, is doubted to be too true; that a main cause of all the misery and mischief in our land is the fearfullest of flattery of our prelates and clergy. The hope of a crosier staff or a cardinal's hat could make many a scholar in England beat his brain to reconcile the Church of Rome and England." [68] The feeling took hold in the public mind that religion would be destroyed because of the Spanish bride. The zeal of the Puritans had its effect, and an opponent retrospectively acknowledged their success on this issue when he wrote that "the ecclesiastic and civil moles cast up so many loose and black suspicions, that he was thought no good protestant that did not think that protestantism was not like to be undermined." [69] The Infanta of Spain was another shibboleth of English Protestantism.

The Infanta was intended to be consort to the Prince of Wales, and it was necessary that the Prince and his father be made to see this bride as a hazard to nation and religion and as a danger to the crown of England. The Infanta in England was seen as a device by which the King would be-

67. PRO SP 14/150/54, 56, 105.
68. Birch, *James I*, II, 392.
69. Warwick, *Memoirs*, 3.

come divided from his people. In Parliament, pamphlet, and pulpit the fear was voiced that Prince and King under subtle Spanish practices might alter their political or religious views, withdraw from the true religion, turn to persecuting the loyal Puritans. Then England would be divided from its King; then Spain would profit from an England of torn allegiances.[70] A Spanish wife for Charles might alienate him from his subjects, but the Puritan had no doubts that such "an Athaliah" would certainly alienate God from the Prince. Alexander Leighton warned his future sovereign with language appropriate for an Elijah admonishing an Ahab: "As for you Gracious Prince: If you desire to present your selfe to God, as a member of his unspotted Spouse in Christ, be not unequally yoked; away with that Lincie-wolsie Match: (with reverence be it spoken) it is a beastly, greasie, and a lowsie-wearing, unbefitting your Grace. Scripture will apologie my termes, which speaking of spirituall whoredome, giveth it alwaies the vilest termes." [71]

Thomas Alured added more Old Testament cases of marriage with idolaters; then, as if to draw a parallel, he cited instances in which English royalty had been unfortunate with Spain: the Black Prince poisoned, Prince Arthur's sudden death, Queen Mary's loss of Calais.[72] The soul of Charles would be jeopardized by this heretical alliance, and there was a further certainty that a Spanish marriage foretold an early death. D'Ewes explained: "The reason why all good Protestants and loyal subjects so feared this match, proceeded from their love to God, his truth, the King and the Prince. For all men knew the Jesuits to be the sworn instruments of the Spanish King, and would easily bring to pass, by poison or otherwise, the abortive ends of our King and Prince,

70. *Commons Debates 1621*, II, 488–492; D'Ewes, I, 158–159; *CSPD, James I*, X, 483; PRO SP 14/142/22.

71. Leighton, *Speculum Belli sacri*, 208.

72. PRO SP 14/115/67.

after he should once have two or three children by the Spanish lady, who, then overliving them, would be sure to train up her offspring in the Romish religion, to the utter ruin of this flourishing Church and Kingdom . . ." [73] The personal danger to Charles and the Spanish danger to England and the English Church came from the proposed marriage with the Infanta of Spain. The Infanta of Spain was the example and the focus of the Spanish threat to England.

Charles did not marry the Spanish Infanta, but the failure was neither his nor the King's. The Spaniards simply had no intention to marry with English heretics. The Puritan thunderings had in no way deterred James or Charles, but the propaganda flood had affected the general English public. It had been fully informed and fully aroused at what the Puritans had conceived to be a Spanish assault on England. The fact that Charles and Buckingham had been vigorous in pushing for the Spanish match was forgotten for a time by a public which made heroes of the errant cavaliers. A moan of despair became a shout of joy. In sermons of thanksgiving, in pamphlets of praise, and in private diaries Puritans acknowledged God's intervention in England's deliverance from the Infanta of Spain and all that she represented.[74] The public celebrated in its own way with bells, bonfires, and liquor. No matter the means of celebration, the cause for celebration was the same: "Wee welcomed his returne with the joyfull shout that attends a Prince from the mouthes of his faithfullest servants; and this was still the foote of our songe of thanksgiving, God be prayesed that he is come home ALONE." [75] Behind the immediate cause for celebration were

73. D'Ewes, I, 182–183.

74. Samuel Ward, *A Peace Offering To God For the Blessings we enjoy under his Majesties reigne, with a Thanksgiving for the Princes safe returne on Sunday the 5. of October. 1623* (London, 1624); Scott, *Vox Dei*, 58–70 *passim; The Diary of Walter Yonge*, 78; Vicars, *Englands Hallelu-jah*, stanzas 42–59.

75. Scott, *Vox Dei*, 63.

all the Puritan efforts to arouse the English public against the Spanish menace of an Infanta of Spain; the national jubilation which greeted the Prince's return was the measure of Puritan success.[76]

The Cruel Spaniard

"I doe beseech the Lord to shew mercy to my native Country, that they may never come under the government of the Spaniards . . . Amen." [77] What were these Spaniards who had attacked England in Queen Elizabeth's day and who now again threatened England? The Puritans warned that Spain bore a religious and national enmity to England. They showed the past examples of Spanish designs against England, and they displayed the contemporary external and internal Spanish assaults on England and the Church of England. But there was something more. There was the Spaniard, and the Spaniard was something unusual, something terrifying. He was the cruel Spaniard.

Spanish cruelty was so frequent a theme in sermon and pamphlet that many Englishmen must have had frightening expectations of their fate at the hands of the Spaniards. These expectations were enforced by the lively recitations of examples of Spanish cruelties to other peoples. In grim detail the Spanish torturings and slaughterings of Indians were described. Should the butchering of distant heathens not evoke a fearful response from the English, they were also presented with the tales of Spanish barbarity against the religious brethren in the Netherlands and in Germany. These examples were near and vivid, and the purpose in

76. Davies, *Huntington Library Quarterly,* 3 (October 1939), 13.

77. S. O., *An Adioynder of Sundry other particular wicked plots and cruel, inhumane, perfidious, yea, unnatural practices of the Spaniards* (n. p., 1624), 14.

displaying these horrors was manifested: "The ripping up of women, the shamefull abusing of them, not to be named, the torturing of men with new devised torments; the bathing in the bloud of inoffensive children; the cruel murthering of Gods Ministers . . . would put life in a man to fight to the last gaspe, rather then to live and see the least part of these horrible indignities." The English were reminded by examples from the recent past and from present reality what savagery would be inflicted upon them as a result of Spanish victory.[78]

Lest the English think that for some reason they would find the Spaniard less cruel, they were given assurances that the terrors to which they had been made witnesses would inevitably follow from a Spanish triumph. England was warned that such brutalities could not be avoided, for cruelty was inherent in the Spaniard's nature. Spaniards were said to relish cruelty, to crave blood; and Scott put his English view of the Spaniard into a Spaniard's speech: "Crueltie (replied Gonzales) is naturall and inhaerent to our Nation, for except our victories be drowned in blood, we cannot taste them."[79] Although a part of Spanish cruelty was attributed to the Romish religion, which often was charged with a bloody record, some preachers asserted that the quality and quantity of the Spanish blood lust was uniquely Spanish. Unnatural cruelty was natural for a Spaniard.[80]

The picture of the Spaniard that was drawn for the Eng-

78. Hampton, *A Proclamation of Warre*, 24–30; T[homas] T[aylor], *A Mappe of Rome: Lively Exhibiting Her Merciles Meeknes and cruell mercies to the Church of God* (London, 1634), 13–14. These sermons were preached on the anniversary of Gunpowder Plot, and they were published several times after 1619. S. O., *An Adioynder*, 2–14; Scott, *A Second Part of Spanish Practises*, the third section entitled "An Ajoynder." The quotation is from Leighton, *Speculum Belli sacri*, 182–183.

79. Scott, *Second Part of Vox Populi*, 48.

80. Robert Jenison, *The Height of Israels Heathenish Idolatrie, In sacrificing their children to the Devill* (London, 1621), 58–63; Taylor, *A Mappe of Rome*, 14–15; Hampton, *A Proclamation of Warre*, 24.

lish public was composed of everything productive of hate and fear. Greed, heresy, treachery, and cruelty marked the Spaniard in such a manner that he appeared to be almost subhuman, or, if not subhuman, at least non-European. Scott had a Spaniard pronounce the taint: "But quoth the Duke of Hyaz, it may be they hate us for the same cause, that France, Germany, Italie, and the rest of the Countries of Europe, for that many of us are discended of the Moorish race . . ."[81] And in the same year of 1624, the year when English hatred and fear of Spain reached a zenith, an anonymous writer apostrophized:

> O honored England, how art thou disgrac't
> With Morish faces thus to be outfac't.[82]

Thus, the element of race was added to the Spaniard's portrait; and for England there could be no mercy from the cruel Spaniard who was, in fact, a Moor.

Clearly, Spain was the enemy in every sense of the word. Imperial in design, hostile in religion, alien in race, Spain was shown to England in the way a catalogue of hates and fears might be displayed. Romish Spain was treacherous, deceitful, heretical; Moorish Spain was cruel beyond comparison. This Spain was again attacking England and true religion, and internal underminings aided its external assault. England was shown how the Spanish attack was made and what savagery would surely follow England's defeat or surrender; for in spite of any appearances of peace, any semblances of friendship or neutrality, England must see that at all times and in all ways Spain was the enemy.

81. Scott, *Second Part of Vox Populi*, 13.
82. PRO SP 14/118/104.

IV

The Dutch

The Bulwark

The religious brethren in Germany were the persecuted Children of God, and as such they were objects of profound sympathy for the Puritans; the Spaniards, the cruel persecutors and cunning enemy, were the spawn of Antichrist, and as such they were feared and hated by the Puritans. The Dutch, sharing a Calvinist heritage with the distressed of Germany and the Puritans of England, shared also their Spanish enemy. Unlike England, where, to the dismay of the Puritans, the government of James and then Charles often declined to see or face the Spanish threat, the Dutch had no alternative to fighting the Spaniard at the gate. The United Provinces stood as a besieged fortress of the religion, a fortress that was not only a haven for the homeless but a bulwark that, by standing firm against Spanish aggression, protected England.

The Dutch, in that they were professors of the true religion, were a nation sanctified unto the Lord, and their land was a Sanctuary of the Lord. A speaker in the Parliament of 1624 explained to his countrymen the foundation of Dutch successes when he called the Dutch "those whome god hath by miracle raysed and supported, who have beene the only remora of the Spaniards greatenes over the Christian world . . ." [1] God had raised them, and it followed that God would favor them. When Walter Yonge noted the floods that enforced the withdrawal of Spinola from before Breda, he wrote that "no hand of man removed him, but God himself." [2] And the English, who saw God raise the United Provinces to oppose Spain's pride and who beheld the miracles performed to uphold the Dutch, prayed that this Sanctuary of the Lord would continue to be saved from the Spanish fury.[3]

The Netherlands had to be denied to the forces of Antichrist for its own sake as a Sanctuary of the Lord, but this place was also the sanctuary of the exiled brethren. In those provinces sheltered remnants of the shattered and persecuted Church. In the safety of the Netherlands there was "a hiding place for the pore persecuted members of Christ hunted out of Bohemia, the Palatinate, and other distressed Countries"; nor was it forgotten that there, too, Elizabeth of Bohemia, the Princess of England, and her hopeful children were given protection and support.[4] The English Puritans saw in the

1. Gurney MS, "1624," 58.

2. *Diary of Walter Yonge*, 77.

3. *The Fairfax Correspondence*, ed. George W. Johnson (2 vols.; London, 1848), I, 313; William Gouge, *The Saints Sacrifice: Or A Commentarie on the CXVI Psalme* (London, 1632), 281–283.

4. [Thomas Scott], *The Belgicke Pismire: Stinging the slothfull Sleeper, and Awaking the Diligent to Fast, Watch, Pray; and Worke Out Their Owne Temporall and Eternall Salvation With Feare and Trembling* (London, 1622), 8 (source of quotation); Winchilsea MS, "1624," fol. II.

United Provinces the gathered fragments of the Palatinate cause — a cause in which many Englishmen had invested with sympathy and interest. Moreover, the Puritans knew that the enemy that had broken the Palatinate and forced Elizabeth of Bohemia into exile was the enemy the Dutch were fighting.

German refugees and the English Princess would find no shortage of Englishmen in the Netherlands, for some of the more zealous and outspoken English found it necessary to put themselves beyond the reach of their unsympathetic government. Preachers came, and there were congregations to hear sermons that were punishable in England. Pamphleteers came, and there were presses to print what they wrote, and there were ways to send the pamphlets into England while permitting at least writer and publisher to remain free of England's laws.[5] In fact, so many things about the Netherlands seemed to please the Puritans that their loyalty to the King of England was questioned.[6] Perhaps some exiles in the Netherlands wavered in their loyalty to the King; nevertheless, in the manner of exiles, their loyalty to their native country remained fixed. In 1640 an English preacher spoke from this sanctuary in the Netherlands to his English congregation, and he admonished them: "pray for all the Churches, pray for Germany, the first place of reformation, pray for Holland your hiding place, and in all your prayers forget not England, still pray for England . . ."[7]

The Neglected Ally

Although the Dutch professed the Calvinist faith and protected the Calvinist refugees of Germany, the Puritans, because of the erratic course of England's official policy, were compelled to inform the English public about the ties

5. *CSPD, Charles I,* VIII, 151, XIII, 518; Wright, *Huntington Library Quarterly,* 6 (February 1943), 153.

6. *CSPD, Charles I,* III, 544.

7. Bridge, *The true Souldiers Convoy,* 69.

that bound England to the Netherlands. Naturally, the Puritans felt that England's most important bond with the Dutch was the religious bond which also joined them in a fellowship with the persecuted of Germany. Robert Jenison, Puritan divine of Newcastle, spoke of this religious connection in its largest sense when he reminded his townsmen that "they there of the reformed Churches especially, are our brethren, & wee members with them of the same body mystical." [8] In Parliament the "one faith" England shared with the Dutch and others was asserted to be the soundest foundation for alliance, for "the firmest band of harts is religion, and theay of the same religion are surest freinds." [9] So strongly did the Puritans feel the religious tie that Scott even reasoned that the English soldiers who came to fight under the Dutch in the cause of religion could fight and die with the comfort of having served England.[10] Because union in the true Church provided the most substantial basis for an alliance between two nations, England was urged to apply a religious criterion to the choice of allies, and Englishmen were encouraged to assist religion and England by fighting for the Dutch.

Nor did the Puritans neglect to remind their countrymen that alliance with the Dutch had some justifications other than similarity of religion. Once again Queen Elizabeth was invoked to establish by the authority of her legendary successes the rightness of a proposal. She spoke again to her people through the medium of a heavenly debate in which Scott employed her to tell the English how she was grieved to see the Dutch lacking England's assistance in the fight

8. Robert Jenison, *Newcastles Call, To her Neighbour and Sister Townes and Cities throughout the land, to take warning by her Sins and Sorrowes* (London, 1637), 2-3.

9. *Commons Debates 1621*, III, 350.

10. [Thomas Scott], *Symmachia: or, A True-Loves Knot. Tyed, Betwixt Great Britaine and the United Provinces . . . For the Weale and Peace of Christendome* (n. p. [Utrecht?], n.d. [1624?]), 18-19.

against Spain.[11] In another pamphlet the Elizabethan hero, Essex, was conjured up in order that he, too, might voice the experience of a glorious era. Essex warned: "Againe, in any wise beware of dis-uniting your selves from the united States of the Netherlands: for it will be to your infinite disadvantage so to do: But rather, assist, cherish, and hearten them: They are the best Confederates you have." [12] By these devices the sanctity of the Elizabethan past was added to the religious bond to build a stronger case for the Dutch alliance. And the unfavorable comparison of the present with the past was sadly echoed by Sir John Eliot in the Parliament of 1629 when he lamented that "our fathers yu know were happie, & we have seene felicity our selves, soe lat it was amongst us, when all our neighbours tooke comforte in our frindships . . ." [13]

Finally, two Puritans mentioned one other bond between England and the Netherlands. Scott in a published tract and D'Ewes in a private letter commented on the similarity of language. D'Ewes, the cautious antiquarian, went no further than to observe that the English and Dutch might have had the same language at one time, but Scott, the zealous polemicist, believed the Dutch to "come of the same race originally that wee doe, as our speech witnesseth . . ." [14] Having in common an original language, the Dutch and the English were held to be of the same race; they were brothers in religion and blood. In contrast, it should be remembered, the Spaniards were looked upon as heretics in religion and non-European in race; and in every way that the Spaniard was different from the Englishman the Dutchman was like the Englishman. Friend and foe were distinguished by faith, actions, and blood.

11. Scott, *Vox Coeli*, 30–31, 43.
12. Scott, *Essex His Ghost*, 16.
13. Eliot, *Negotium Posterorum*, II, 134–135.
14. D'Ewes, II, 182; Scott, *The Belgicke Pismire*, 49.

The Puritans were forced to underline those ties of religion, history, and race that joined England with the Netherlands because they feared that the English government had chosen to neglect the Dutch alliance. The government, they claimed, was not supporting the Dutch in their conflict with Spain, a conflict in which a Dutch failure would imperil the continued existence of Protestantism. While James allowed the Spaniards to talk him into disgraceful political impotency, the stout Dutch fought for the Church without the traditional assistance of England. The Puritans, undeceived by Spanish tricks, knew Spain was the real threat, and therefore they wanted England to help rather than ignore the Dutch in their struggle against this Spanish enemy.[15] Because the Dutch battle against Spain was the Church's battle against Antichrist, the attitude taken by Englishmen in regard to aiding the Netherlands was used to provide another mark of identification for the Puritan, and one writer even made this identification explicit:

A Puritan is hee that rather had
Spend all to helpe the States, hee is so mad
Then spend one hundred thousand pound a yeare
to guard the Spanish coasts from Pyrats feare,
The whilst the Catholique King might force combine
Both Holland, Beame, & Paltz to undermine.[16]

Worse than the charge of England's neglect of the Dutch was the accusation that England was actually undermining the Dutch bulwark by urging the United Provinces to conclude a peace with Spain. The Dutch were no longer to war against the Spaniard; instead they were to follow England's

15. Gurney MS, "1624," 103–105; D'Ewes, I, 22, II, 182.
16. Scott, *The Interpreter*, 3. "Beame" and "Paltz" are Bohemia and the Palatinate.

unwise course of treating with Spain, which so dearly loved the cheap victory gained from negotiations.[17]

Spain, the Puritans warned, was the sole gainer from England's hazardous treatment of its strongest and most faithful ally.[18] By forsaking the Dutch, by undermining them with dangerous treaties, England was only aiding the Spanish attempt to break that Dutch bulwark which helped to protect England from Spanish assault. Who in England, the Puritan might have asked, sought to rupture this necessary alliance between England and the Netherlands? Who desired the ruin of the Dutch brethren and the triumph of the cruel Spaniard? In 1624 this answer was published: "There is a Spanishsied popish pamphleteer, endeavouring to maligne the State of the United Provinces (erected & maintayned by the finger of God) who disswadeth all men from maintenance, protection, and partaking of, and with the Hollanders . . ."[19] In 1639 they were "the Papists and Spanish faction, who . . . do labour with all the might they can to cause a breach between us and Holland, a greater mischief than which there cannot be . . . those profane knaves who hate honest Protestants whom they now term Puritans . . ."[20] Here too, where England jeopardized itself by neglecting the Dutch ally, the danger was encouraged by the English Catholics, who favored the imperial designs of Spain. The Protestant Englishman was known by his desire to support the Dutch, while the Catholic Englishman was known by his desire to neglect the Dutch and thereby assist the cruel Spaniard.

The Example to England

Those in England who complained of the government's dangerous neglect of the Dutch bulwark also offered the

17. Scott, *Vox Coeli*, 30–31; PRO SP 16/173/49.
18. J. R., *The Spy*, sig. E1; Vicars, *Englands Hallelu-jah*, stanza 52.
19. Leighton, *Speculum Belli sacri*, 306.
20. PRO SP 16/431/20.

Dutch to the English public as an example worthy of emulation. In religion, in war, and in commerce the Dutch were successful, and England was told that it could obtain similar successes by following the course of the United Provinces.

Puritan attention to the Dutch example understandably laid stress upon religion, for the Dutch Church was often compared with the English Church. Some comparisons between religion in the Netherlands and in England shamed England. The anonymous defender of Prynne, Burton, and Bastwick condemned the English services and attacked Archbishop Laud for the omission of prayers for the Electoral family; the writer then went on to inform his readers that in the Dutch Church prayers were offered not only for Elizabeth of Bohemia and her children but for the King of England as well.[21] The Dutch Church appeared to shame the English Church by displaying more concern for Protestantism and England's exiled Princess than was allowed to the English by their own Church.

One prayer, no matter how much it told against Laudian ways, did not define differences in religious practices, but the English Puritans noted other Dutch religious observances which they favored for England. The Dutch humiliated themselves with days set aside for public fast and prayer, while the English, although aware of the afflictions of the Church in Germany and the persecution of their Princess, only became more swollen in pomp and pride. The Puritans in England, who objected to the ceremonies, images, and ornaments introduced into the Anglican Church, looked to the Netherlands and prayed for it.[22] England, with its popishly inclined ecclesiastics, could learn from "the plain, plump Hollander . . . who, before any great undertaking, useth not the vain, ostentatious pomp of a procession, but celebrateth a bid-day

21. *Divine and Politike Observations*, 33.
22. Scott, *The Belgicke Pismire*, 88–89; PRO SP 16/261/F, 206–207.

or a general fast"; and if England desired the blessings heaped upon the Dutch, it would do well to follow the Dutch example in religion.[23]

One such blessing bountifully given to the Dutch was military success, for with the strong foundation of true religion and a firm adherence to their faith the Dutch were assured of victory in war. Furthermore, the Dutch, who fought from the strength of their religion, knew that in combating the merciless Spaniard they were openly fighting for their lives and their religion. They knew their real enemy was Spain; and, unlike an unwilling England, the Dutch fought in the Lord's battle against Antichrist.[24] Although the Puritans praised the Dutch for knowing and fighting the real enemy, the aim of this praise was to show Englishmen what must be done. When Scott remarked how quickly the English became more proficient than the Dutch in the use of arms once they resolved to learn from the Dutch example, he was encouraging his countrymen to further emulation.[25] English pride was saved, for the Englishman could be confident that would he but take some lessons from his Dutch ally he soon would be the teacher.

There was one more lesson that the English could learn as a consequence of observing the Dutch example in war:

> The dutch man shudars hele now have warrs with
> spayne
> and share with him who now fills all the mayne
> All all alone melts mountaynes of rich oare
> and lets none breath upon his new worlds shore,

23. Birch, *Charles I,* II, 128, 134.

24. Scott, *The Belgick Souldier,* 36; Leighton, *Speculum Belli sacri,* 182–183; *The Fairfax Correspondence,* I, 261–262; H. P., *Digitus Dei or Good Newes from Holland. Sent to the world* . . . (Rotterdam, 1631), 1–11; Gouge, *The Saints Sacrifice,* 282–283.

25. Scott, *Sir Walter Rawleighs Ghost,* 4.

but by his peace getts mony so to become
to strong and terrible for all christendome.
On gentle Lanes thy unleagred hands sore free,
Doe that alone which we would doe with thee.[26]

England could, by joining the Netherlands in war against
Spain, not only help secure a neglected ally, the Reformed
Church, and England's safety, but could also share in the
spoils now enjoyed only by the Dutch. This kind of proposal
must have appealed to those in England who advocated a return to the Elizabethan naval war against Spain; but the
general prosperity of the Netherlands was used to demonstrate that no matter what type of war was waged, wars
against Spain brought prosperity. The United Provinces, it
was said, had won victories over enormous forces; and while
they were winning those victories for Protestantism, their
wealth at home and their trade abroad had expanded.[27] Riches
could be England's; for wealth in the Dutch manner was a
result of commerce in the Dutch manner, which, in turn, was
a nation's reward when it was faithful to religion and opposed
to religion's enemies. Certainly, the Puritans believed, England should not neglect an ally from whom England had so
much to learn, and the most strenuous Puritan advocate made
that point in a cogent statement: "All that I have said is to
this end, to leade you by the hand to the Pismire of the united
Provinces, that considering her wayes and course aright . . .
wee may by her example, and Salomons instruction, grow
wiser then we are, though we fall short of what we ought to
be." [28]

The Puritans pictured the Netherlands standing against

26. *Commons Debates 1621*, VI, 188. These are the first eight lines of an
eighteen-line poem which concludes the notes on the Parliament of 1621 by
Sir Thomas Holland.
27. Scott, *The Belgick Souldier*, 29–37.
28. Scott, *The Belgicke Pismire*, 47.

the forces of Catholic Spain as a Protestant bulwark, which was itself a part of the Reformed Church, which sheltered remnants of the distressed German Churches, and which also helped to guard England from Spanish assaults. However, the English Puritans saw their own government neglect the Dutch alliance in such a way as to weaken the bulwark and thereby endanger England. Against this mistreatment of England's most important ally the Puritans vigorously objected, and they went on to propose that England take an example from the Dutch. In the Dutch example the Puritans asked England to behold a nation with a more completely reformed Church, more nationally devoted to religion, more truly committed to the protection and advancement of Protestantism, and more successful and prosperous. On each of these points the Dutch were a standard of comparison against which England was required to measure itself. Nevertheless, the Puritans did not see the Dutch as the ultimate embodiment of the best. In many ways better than England, the Dutch were not perfect. There was, in fact, another picture of the Dutch.

Conflicts

An appraisal of Puritan thought that relied upon Puritan attitudes to foreign nations would discover that the English Puritans did not believe that anything temporal could be wholly good. There was perfect evil in the world; the Puritans saw the perfect evil that was the Antichrist and his legions in the shape of Catholic Spain, to which no good attribute was ever applied. But there was no perfectly good nation to stand opposite the perfect evil of Spain. Probably the Dutch came nearest to the ideal of a good nation: they were almost constantly warring against the earthly Antichrist;

they were most often held up to England as an example of more complete reformation; they were blessed by apparently divine miracles. The Netherlands was not, however, a nation of perfect good, and the Puritans found failings in their Dutch brethren. The English observed some religious and national weaknesses in the Dutch — weaknesses which not only conflicted with the idea of a good nation but produced real and dangerous political conflicts with England.

Failures in what might be called the Dutch national character generated difficulties with England and necessarily troubled the English Puritans. The Puritan admirers of the Dutch sometimes found themselves in the embarrassing position of advocating stronger friendship with an ally who irritated the English government and even angered the English public by antagonistic actions. Nevertheless, the Puritans knew and declared that the only benefit to be gained by conflict between these imperfect, but Protestant, allies was the benefit derived by the perfect enemy — Spain. That terrible consideration forced the English Puritans to defend or excuse, as often as it was possible, those faults in the Dutch that could create a rupture in the Anglo-Dutch alliance. Whatever the problem, it had to be smoothed over in order not to leave the Dutch bulwark unsupported by England.

Amboyna

Puritan efforts to preserve amity between England and the Netherlands faced a severe test in 1623 when the Dutch tortured and executed ten Englishmen at the factory of Amboyna in the East Indies. Conflict between the two East India companies had become chronic; the English, who were weak in that region, usually lost and usually attempted to enlist the support of the King. Hence, commercial frictions often threatened to involve governments and nations. But the massacre at Amboyna was more than another trade problem: the Dutch had shed English blood, and England had been insulted. Earlier complaints by the East India Company to the English government swelled into the anger of a nation aroused over a disgrace inflicted by a supposedly friendly ally.[29]

England's East India Company complained vigorously about the execution of its men. The Company, charging that the massacre had been planned in Amsterdam to ruin it and force the abandonment of its trade, demanded justice.[30] The Company did not satisfy itself with demands; it also took steps to inform and, it was feared, arouse the English public. A painter was hired to produce "a detailed picture of all the tortures inflicted on the English at Amboyna," and a play on the same subject was commissioned. Although the Dutch representatives in London, apprehensive of a riot, were able to have the Council suppress the play and the picture, they and the Council failed to prevent the publication of some pamphlets obviously inspired by the English East India Company.[31] At first a moderate book was offered to the public with the explanation that the Company was being careful not to do anything that might increase the tension between the two countries.[32] This kindly impulse was repressed when a piece of inflammatory propaganda was printed. The tract, *The Stripping of Joseph,* had a curious genesis, for it was originally an old sermon without any reference to the Dutch. However, the sermon's theme fitted the occasion, and Thomas Myriell, pastor of St. Stephen Walbrook, refurbished it with

29. PRO SP 14/111/126–127; Gardiner, V, 242–243; Pieter Geyl, *The Netherlands in the Seventeenth Century,* Part One, 1609–1648 (New York, 1961), 87, 173–180.

30. PRO SP 14/168/48.

31. The quotation is from Chamberlain, *Letters,* 601–602; PRO SP 14/184/22.

32. *A True Relation of the Uniust, Cruell, and Barbarous Proceedings against the English at Amboyna In the East-Indies by the Neatherlandish Governour and Councel there* (London, 1624), "To the Reader."

a violent dedicatory epistle in which the attack by the Dutch was asserted to be even worse than Spanish cruelty. The condition which made the Dutch worse than the Spaniards was given in a series of questions:

> But, O then, what shall we say to them who being of the same Religion, and upon termes of peace, have practised most exquisite torments upon the innocent bodies of their Friends and Confederates?
>
> . . . . .
>
> But, O unkinde, unnaturall! You this to us? We this from you? Whilst the Blood of our valiant Countrimen lies reeking on the ground, to keepe you in your owne Land, doe you wastefully spill the blood of our faithfull Countrimen in a strange Land? O more then Scythian barbarisme. Doe you so requite us? [33]

The evil committed by a friend was more painful than the evil of an avowed enemy; when propaganda was added to the deed itself, the popular reaction against the friend was at least painful and sometimes violent. In a letter a student at Emmanuel College, Cambridge described the massacre as "most barbarous" and felt that one of the books written about it "will breed a generall distast if not enmity betweene us and them." [34] This "distast" was expressed by other Englishmen who fought (and were often killed) in quarrels about the Dutch actions at Amboyna, or who appeared so near rioting against the Dutch in London that the government ordered

33. Robert Wilkinson, *The Stripping of Joseph, Or The crueltie of Brethren to a Brother . . . With a Consolatorie Epistle, to the English-East-India Companie, for their unsufferable wrongs susstayned in Amboyna, by the Dutch there. Published and presented unto them, by Tho. Myriell. Pastor of Saint Stephens in Walbrooke* (London, 1625), 10–12.

34. *The Oxinden Letters, 1607–1642*, ed. Dorothy Gardiner (London, 1933), 18.

an extra eight hundred men to stand watch on Shrove Tuesday in 1625. But the English reaction that was most dangerous to the alliance was not expressed in tavern brawls or holiday riots, both of which were indigenous to the English scene; the reaction most dangerous to the Dutch was that "they have almost lost the hearts of their best friends here . . ." John Chamberlain, usually well-disposed towards the Netherlands, wanted England to take vengeance by seizing Dutch ships and summarily hanging some of the crews.[35] When those in England who ordinarily favored the United Provinces were moved that deeply, the controversy would not be easily forgotten. Nor was it. In 1628 the King had to order Attorney General Heath to suppress more writings about Amboyna, and in 1631 two Englishmen serving the Emperor killed seventeen Hollanders to avenge the death of a kinsman at Amboyna.[36]

With reactions in England running strong, any apologist for the Netherlands faced a task of unenviable difficulty. Still, no Puritan could rightly ignore his calling, and the calling of political pamphleteer was on Thomas Scott, who raised a lonely and worried voice in favor of the Dutch and continued Anglo-Dutch amity. The pre-Amboyna conflicts, which had arisen out of commercial competition in the East Indies and elsewhere, had been serious enough to make Scott attempt an explanation of them. This served as a kind of practice for Amboyna, but it can also be seen as an excellent example of the man's fine mastery of propaganda techniques. To excuse the Dutch, Scott attacked their accusers, who were identified as those formalist English Protestants who would appease Spain and do nothing for true Protestantism.[37] Simi-

---

35. PRO SP 14/172/17, I, 18; Chamberlain, *Letters,* 601–602, 569–570 (the quotation is from 601–602).

36. *CSPD, Charles I,* III, 401–402; Birch, *Charles I,* II, 109–110.

37. Scott, *The Interpreter,* 8.

larly, the Dutch who offered injuries to the English merchants were not acting for the United Provinces; they were wicked individuals, "mungrell Spaniards in affection, and perhaps in blood . . ."[38]

Nevertheless, no amount of practice at smoothing over trade frictions could fully prepare Scott to cope with the outcry raised over Amboyna. He devoted an entire work to re-tying "A True-Loves Knot" between England and the Nether-lands, but he obviously found the job difficult. He and other Puritans usually maintained that the United Provinces was England's bulwark; yet when Amboyna compelled him to ad-monish the Dutch in some manner, he was forced into the contradictory position of warning that "it were an ingratefull part in them, whilst wee indanger our selves by houlding up theire chinnes, to keepe them from sincking, that they s'hould with their heeles kick us under water." Here, too, he proposed and accepted the explanation that removed the fault from the States and placed it on private persons. At the end of the pamphlet he even suggested that a part of the wrong might have been the fault of the Englishmen involved, and he con-cluded with the prayer that censure by either side be with-held until the incident was impartially examined.[39] In another work Scott returned to his permanent theme when he pointed where the guilt might be placed by an impartial examination: "For I verily beleeve, that that disgust betwixt the two Na-tions in the East-Indies, was not sent thither without a

38. [Thomas Scott], *A Tongue-Combat, Lately Happening Betweene two English Souldiers in the Tilt-boat of Gravesend, The One Going to Serve the King of Spaine, the other to serve the States Generall of the United Provinces* . . . (London, 1623), 69. The English East India Company at first seemed inclined to blame the massacre at Amboyna on individual Dutchmen, but at least some of the public refused to accept that explanation and squarely condemned the Netherlands. See *A True Relation* and Chamberlain, *Letters,* 569–570.

39. Scott, *Symmachia,* 2 (source of the quotation), 3–11, 34.

Romish practise . . ." [40] Once again the enemy of both the Dutch and the English was found stirring up trouble between the Protestant allies; and, by casting the blame for Amboyna upon individuals or enemy plotters, Scott tried to modify the shock in England and realign English sentiment with the polestars of hatred to Spain and friendship with the Dutch. His burden was heavy, and it was to his credit that he alone of the Puritan advocates for the Dutch was neither provoked to anger nor stunned into silence by the massacre at Amboyna.

Other Conflicts

The massacre at Amboyna was the most spectacular conflict of this period between England and the United Provinces, for it seriously strained the generally favorable impression of the Dutch held by many in England. Although Amboyna produced the most vocal reactions in England, those reactions must be placed within the context of a persistent undercurrent of English criticisms, which often were responses to Anglo-Dutch conflicts. These criticisms of the Dutch were not always Puritan criticisms; to the contrary, the attacks can sometimes be seen in the Puritan attempts to answer the charges of other Englishmen against the Dutch ally. As in the response to Amboyna, English Puritans occasionally concurred in the disapproval of certain Dutch faults, but the Puritans also saw other Dutch failings that were of special brotherly interest to them. Generally then, English complaints about the Dutch were concerned either with national conflicts or religious defects, and usually the Puritans attempted to mollify the former while remarking on the latter.

The inevitable national irritations which developed from the trade rivalry of the two maritime countries not only produced the explosive hatred after Amboyna but constituted

40. Scott, *The Belgicke Pismire,* 67.

an area of constant rubs and potential new Amboynas. The English beheld their Dutch ally prospering while, it was thought, England's commerce was declining. This spectacle was made no easier for the Englishman by the ruthless Dutch trading methods, which seemed calculated to affront English traders and the English government. In the Indies, Greenland, Muscovy, and the Narrow Seas the Dutch merchants and fishermen elbowed their English counterparts and roughly ignored English protests. Scott could claim the frictions were exaggerated by certain nominal Protestants in England, but in 1622 even he acknowledged a wish for Dutch amendment of the commercial quarrels. But amendment that might be less profitable was not favored by the Dutch, who in 1631 responded to an English complaint with a reminder that the English could expect no satisfaction for this lesser matter when they (the Dutch) had succeeded in ignoring English protests about Amboyna.[41] Trade rivalry and fishing quarrels were commercial conflicts that could be kept external, but the Dutch were also said to be responsible for an internal commercial problem caused by an outflow of bullion from England. Again, even Scott admitted to some justice in this complaint, but he chose to emphasize that more of England's coin was sent out of the country by the Catholics, who deceitfully blamed the Dutch.[42] Nevertheless, apologies for the Dutch, no matter how ingenious, could not hide the real commercial conflicts between the two nations, and those conflicts did not further that Anglo-Dutch concord so dear to Puritan thinking.

Dutch commercial avarice was the most important and dangerous, but not the only, national character fault that annoyed the English public and created difficulties for the English

41. George Edmundson, *Anglo-Dutch Rivalry, 1600–1653* (Oxford, 1911), 34; Chamberlain, *Letters,* 424; Scott, *The Interpreter,* 9; *CSPD, Charles I,* V, 209.

42. Scott, *Vox Populi,* sig. C4, and *A Tongue-Combat,* 70–71.

Puritans. Ingratitude to England was added to avarice in the negative picture of the Netherlands; and although Scott, ever sensitive to any criticism of the Dutch, claimed that the charge of ingratitude was brought by "profest Enemies," he was forced to this explanation: "And if the Netherlands should say (as you report) that we tooke their parts partly for our owne sakes, they should say nothing but truth, and it concernes us so to doe; yet this diminisheth not the cause of their gratitude . . ."[43] Also, when the Dutch, who were supposed to be England's martial tutors, did not perform too well in the field, at least one Englishman was keen to make cowardice a part of the Dutch character.[44] Finally, frugality must be counted among the miscellaneous national defects, for it was the Dutchmen's characteristic frugality that made them somewhat neglectful of the interests of religion.[45]

Where the Puritans ignored or excused most Dutch failings of national character, they were foremost in correcting any faults that weakened true religion. In religion the Dutch were an example to England, but Dutch practice was not always perfect, and they and the English were warned not to presume on God's toleration of their religious imperfections.[46] In a sense the Puritans by pointing out Dutch errors were only performing the obligations of loving brothers, and this type of criticism followed the general Puritan pattern of being aware of English criticisms and conflicts with the Dutch but preferring to excuse, explain, or moderate any difficulties with the United Provinces.

Typical of that moderate Puritan approach to criticism of the Dutch bulwark was Puritan comment on the observance of the Sabbath in the Netherlands. Alexander Leighton

43. Scott, *The Belgicke Pismire,* 10, and *A Tongue-Combat,* 66.
44. D'Ewes, II, 169–170. This observation was made in a letter from W. Beeston to D'Ewes.
45. *CSPD, Charles I,* VI, 439; Scott, *The Belgicke Pismire,* 9.
46. Leighton, *Speculum Belli sacri,* 119–121.

gave his view: "This sin cryes in England; and roares in Holland, where by open shops, and other works of their calling, they proclaim, with open mouth, their little regard of God, or his Sabboth." A few pages later he again mentioned Sabbath-breaking: "I wish to God that the United Provinces, and all others that professe the Gospell, would looke to this." [47] It is important to notice here that although Leighton was condemning the Dutch for their profanations of the Sabbath, his comments were not confined exclusively to them. By joining England with the Netherlands in the practice of this sin, the Dutch example, imperfect as it was, was still sustained.

Another fault of the Dutch was marked by the Puritans in much the same way. Leighton and Scott mildly accused them of neglecting their ministers. Scott complained that the clergy in the Netherlands were insufficiently rewarded by the frugal Dutch, while Leighton wanted them to pay more attention to their ministers and thereby do as much for the service of God as they did for themselves.[48] Implied were two of the national criticisms — frugality and ingratitude — but the Puritans, when they found faults in the Dutch, approached the defects through religion and with considerable moderation.

Although there was no moderation in the Puritan's fierce hatred of Arminianism in England, in this period there seems to have been a notable lack of Puritan attention to Arminianism in the country of its origin. In the third Parliament of Charles I the point was made that the Arminians, "having kindled a fire in our neighbor country, now they have brought over some of its hither, to set on flame this Kingdom also." [49] Similarly, in 1631 a minister preached that "Popish darts whet afresh on a Dutch grindstone pierced deep, and without

47. *Ibid.* 267–268, 279.

48. Scott, *The Belgicke Pismire,* 9; Leighton, *Speculum Belli sacri,* 312–313.

49. *Commons Debates 1629,* 13. See also *Notes in Parliament 1628,* 37, and PRO SP 16/142/94.

speedy succour will prove mortal . . ." [50] These instances, however, used the Dutch as a negative example and as a warning to England. Thus even so hated a belief as Arminianism did not at this time create much Puritan criticism of the Netherlands. Perhaps the English Puritans were so involved in urging England's reformation along Dutch lines that it would have been inappropriate to condemn as the homeland of a Protestant heresy the nation they were most concerned to have England emulate.

Dutch Arrogance

For many of the English criticisms of the Dutch there was a root cause in the Dutch character, and that root cause was, in the English view, Dutch arrogance. Arrogance motivated the Dutch offenses against England; arrogance was the source of some of the Dutch offenses against God. Furthermore, this arrogance was the character fault most frequently noticed even by the well-disposed Puritan critics of the United Provinces.

When the English suffered, or thought they suffered, injury and ingratitude from their ally, they were chagrined to find their complaints arrogantly rejected. Where commerce was involved, the Dutch seemed to take a kind of pleasure in insulting the English. In 1621 when a matter of a ship was under negotiation between the two countries, the Dutch attitude to the negotiations provoked this comment from an Englishman: "In truth they begin every day to be descried and decried more and more, and their best frends who for the common considerations of religion and neighborhoode alwayes wisht them well, crie out upon them for the continuall injuries and insolencies we receve from them . . ." [51] The situation had not changed by 1634; when King Charles was

50. PRO SP 16/192/31.
51. Chamberlain, *Letters,* 346.

addressed about Dutch encroachments on English fishing grounds, he was informed that the Dutch were "so insolent that in their jovial meetings they say England will never be well governed until they have the governing of it." [52] Their arrogance toward England was also displayed in matters not involving any commercial conflict. English assistance in the form of soldiers was met with ungrateful scorn, which drew a reproachful admonition from Alexander Leighton.[53] This unfortunate Dutch trait was so noticeable that Sir Robert Phelips, while urging the Parliament of 1621 to aid the United Provinces, had to confess that "ther prids hath swelled of late." [54]

Dutch pride was not solely expressed in their attitude towards England; this same fault was observable in some of their religious attitudes. Sabbath profanation in the Netherlands, by putting personal gain above divine commandment, revealed an arrogance towards God. Nor was Dutch ingratitude for assistance displayed only toward England; God, who made and sustained the Netherlands as a chosen Sanctuary, was not sufficiently remembered as the giver of Dutch victories. "Yea, let those to whom God in fighting of his battles hath given any victory, be humbled for their great neglect of this. I speak in particular to the Hollander, whose deliverances hath been admirable, and whose maintenance is from the very finger of God against the whole forces of Babel; but I fear their forgetfulness wil make God weary of them." [55] God, like England, went unthanked by a self-centered, self-seeking people, whose cardinal fault of arrogance was displayed in many forms and appeared to carry the seeds of possible Dutch self-destruction.

52. *CSPD, Charles I,* VII, 390–391.
53. Leighton, *Speculum Belli sacri,* 279, 312–313.
54. *Commons Debates 1621,* III, 450.
55. Leighton, *Speculum Belli sacri,* 231.

Resolution in Necessity

The picture of the arrogant Dutch placed against the picture of the Dutch bulwark offered a contrast but not a contradiction. The Puritans, of course, were more interested in emphasizing the importance of the Dutch bulwark, but they were cognizant of the other aspects of the Dutch character. Above all conflicts, however, they and some others in England beheld an overriding necessity before which imperfect England's conflicts with an criticisms of an imperfect Netherlands had to be submerged. They had to be submerged in order that the two great Protestant powers could stand together to face the Spanish assaults directed against them both. The peril to the Reformed Church, in some places destroyed, and the peril to Europe, where some nations had been conquered, required the maintenance of the Anglo-Dutch alliance in spite of all disagreements and defects.

Informed Englishmen, who saw both pictures of the Dutch, continued to accept the necessary alliance. When in 1622 Spinola was forced to withdraw from before Bergen, Chamberlain wrote that it "was very welcome newes and as well receved here as came many a day, wherein those people may see our true hearts and goode affection towards them, that howsoever we complaine to have found hard usage at their handes, yet we rejoyce excedingly at their prosperitie and welfare." [56] Even after Amboyna, Samuel Purchas, who was close to the East India Company, wrote that his descriptions of Dutch hostility to the English in the Indies were not intended as condemnations of the Dutch people, who were, after all, coreligionists. Public opinion, in spite of Amboyna and the numerous lesser clashes with the United Provinces, remained

56. Chamberlain, *Letters*, 453–454.

reasonably restrained, even tolerant, of Dutch faults.[57] That this was the case must be credited to the Puritans, who saw and made England see the necessity which resolved the conflicts between the two nations.

Clearly the only nation to derive any benefit from conflicts between England and the Netherlands was Spain, and it was this fact of political life that moved the Puritans to educate their countrymen on the importance of the Dutch bulwark to England. Where Englishmen and Dutchmen might be blind to their own advantage, the Spaniard was not blind to his, for the Spaniard knew it was to his gain to breed trouble between the Protestant allies. Scott phrased the point this way: "The enemye both to our Religion and State seemes to observe this better then our selves; since they have used all endeavors to make breaches betwixt us, and to keepe us off from each other at an unprofitable distance, where the force of our cold amitie could not have powerfull effect to assist each other, or oppose them." [58] A divided Protestantism was a weakened Protestantism, and Spain, by creating and encouraging divisive frictions, weakened formidable opponents. Against a disunited England and Netherlands the Spanish imperial designs could be more swiftly effected; and the goal of those designs, as the Puritans warned, was not just the snuffing out of independence in Spain's former provinces but the conquest of England and the suppression of true religion. All the predicted terrors would come to pass were Spain to be successful in its efforts to have England abandon the Dutch because of conflicts which often were Spanish plots to further Spanish plans.[59]

57. Wright, *Religion and Empire*, 121–122; Edmundson, *Anglo-Dutch Rivalry*, 34.
58. Scott, *Symmachia*, 1. See also Scott, *The Belgicke Pismire*, first page of "To the true-hearted British Readers."
59. *Commons Debates 1621*, III, 450; Scott, *Vox Dei*, second page of "To the Reader"; PRO SP 16/431/20.

The Spaniards, knowing their advantage lay in a collapse of the Anglo-Dutch alliance, worked for that collapse; but in this task they had the invaluable assistance of the Dutch — the arrogant Dutch. Again, it was the observant and informed John Chamberlain who realized where Dutch arrogance was leading the Netherlands and England. He wrote: "for the world here is generally distasted with their proceeding, and their best frends are faln from them seeing theyre perverse, wilfull, and insensat dealing, as yf God had infatuated and blinded their understanding, not to see that they do the Spaniards busines, and that all the world workes to theyre ends more then they could expect or almost wish: but yf yt be in fatis that we shold sincke together who can withstand yt?" [60]

It appeared that the two nations, bound together in many ways, were also bound by the necessity that if one fell they both would fall. To prevent this fall to which Dutch arrogance was contributing, Scott devoted his *Symmachia* to removing the hazardous differences between the allies. In this work of attempted pacification he urged the Dutch to alter their conduct towards England in order that Spain would cease to reap the benefit from quarrels of necessarily dependent friends.[61] Although the Dutch were advised to repent of their actions and arrogance, the English were told that even if there were no desired reformation of Dutch character, the conflicts must be set aside as long as such clashes in any way interfered with the common front against the common enemy. It was far better for England to bear the burden of and ungrateful ally than to bear the yoke of Spanish tyranny.[62]

60. Chamberlain, *Letters*, 424.

61. Scott, *Symmachia*, 1, 11–33 (especially 30).

62. Wilkinson, *The Stripping of Joseph*, 12–18 (part of the epistle written by Myriell); Scott, *The Interpreter*, 9.

Necessity had to resolve the conflicts and prevent any ruptures in the alliance. Ties of race, geography, tradition, and even religion, "the firmest band of harts," joined the two nations, but it was Spain, the common danger, that imposed upon them the necessity to remain bound together.[63] This real necessity to defend nation and religion from the attacks of Spain not only made a break in the alliance impossible but should, in the Puritan view, force England to assist the Dutch bulwark. Thomas Scott, whose hatred of Spain and admiration of the United Provinces led him to wage an untiring propaganda campaign to inform his native England, should be permitted a summary remark: "Assuredly, Necessity calls upon us, to do something in time, for our cause, and our friendes, or to prepare our selves to suffer all thinges from our Enemyes." [64]

63. *Commons Debates 1621*, III, 350, 450.
64. Scott, *Vox Dei,* second page of "To the Reader." Scott's pro-Dutch sentiments and his fictional method did not die with him. In the State Papers for 1640 an anonymous author's letter from the Devil to Rome interpreted as divine intervention Van Tromp's victory over the Spaniards (PRO SP 16/ 539/20).

V

France

The Two Frances

The least readily grasped Puritan view was the attitude towards France. The Palatinate, the Netherlands, and especially Spain created clear impressions for the Puritans; and, because of that clarity of impression, they were generally able to enunciate with some precision what should be England's approach to those countries. There was, however, no fairly simple way to consider France, for France presented the English Puritans with a picture composed of too many ambiguous elements for it to be easily comprehended. There were in a sense two Frances: the contemporary Catholic kingdom that was an ancient rival, and the France of the semi-independent Huguenot community. It might be expected that the Puritan image of Catholic France would approximate their image of Catholic Spain, but that was not at all the case. Instead, the Puritans' view of this aspect of France was more like their picture of the Netherlands, which was imposed by necessity, than their picture of Spain, where unalterable fear and hatred determined the position. The second France, the Protestant minority, was for the English Puritans almost another Palatinate; towards the Huguenots and England's relations with them they responded with some of the same reactions associated with the Palatinate. Assuredly, when the images of the two Frances were combined, the product tended to be uncertain, a trifle out of focus; but this slightly incoherent quality has a value of its own in illuminating the total Puritan attitude towards other nations in this crucial period.

Catholic France

Perhaps the element in the Puritan view that makes that view most difficult to systematize was the neutral impression of Catholic France. Roman religion and Spanish aggression were inseparable and almost synonymous in the Puritan mind; yet that same religion, so hated in a Spaniard, was not offered as a cause of enmity with France. Sir John Eliot, who in Parliament often took the lead in denouncing Catholic Spain, never, according to his most recent biographer, attacked France on religious grounds; in fact, he at no time denounced France.[1] Even the English Catholics, accused of a Spanish loyalty, appeared aware of the difference between France and Spain in English eyes, for one Puritan observed that when the Catholics in London wanted a place to hold services they chose Black Friars next to the house of the French ambassador as being less suspicious to the public than any place identified with Spain.[2]

Nor did the Puritans believe that Catholic France shared Catholic Spain's ambition for world empire, and the threat

1. Harold Hulme, *The Life of Sir John Eliot* (New York, 1957), 65.
2. Scott, *Digitus Dei*, 23.

Spain posed to all nations was not charged against France. France was exonerated and Spain was charged when Scott employed a representation of France to admonish Spain: "for to spoyle the earth of people (as you have done in the Indiaes) and to raign over naked Countreys voyd of inhabitants, is a certaine politick Precept, which is not found in the French reason of State; for I have learned to my cost to content my selfe with a little, so it be good; and therefore I place my gratnesse more in the multitude of Subjects, then in the extent of Kingdomes; and so as my French may live comodiously in this world, I am well pleased that others shall doe so too." [3] So it was that France, a member of the same dreaded religion, was not bound to a Spanish course in the same way that religion served to join England with the United Provinces. Whatever similarities religion should have developed in France to make France like Spain, they were not present. To the English Puritans, France was clearly not Spain.

It was not always clear, however, what France did mean to the Puritans. Some of the remarks about France display a body of opinion that must be denominated a kind of no-comment neutrality. There was certainly an interest in French events, but the expressions of this interest were sometimes so withdrawn and objective that the authors might have been writing about Eskimos rather than about an important nation only a few miles away. Walter Yonge, a Puritan lawyer from Devonshire, made numerous diary references to affairs in France, but nearly all his statements were like news reports. [4] For example, he recorded this without personal comment: "There was a great massacre in France, committed by the

3. [Thomas Scott], *Newes from Pernassus. The Politicall Touchstone, Taken From Mount Pernassus: Whereon the Governments of the greatest Monarchies of the World are touched* (Helicon [Utrecht?], 1622), 38–39.

4. *The Diary of Walter Yonge*, 38–39, 52–54, 65, 80, 84–85, 102, 104–106, 111.

papists upon the Protestants in Brittany." [5] No curses for the malefactors, no prayers for the religious brethren; Yonge simply wrote what had happened in France. Nor was he unique in this, for when in 1626 the French seized English ships and detained the crews, another Englishman described those acts in a straightforward fashion with no expressions of anti-French sentiment. [6]

Thus Catholic France, in contrast to its Catholic neighbor, was perceived with interest; but the interest often was restrained by a curious sense of detachment. There was no feeling of a French threat, nor was there any evidence of feelings of friendship towards France. Rather, the Puritans approached France with an attitude of neutral interest which permitted them to see France as neither a friend nor a foe but as a nation which could be useful to England.

The Ally against Spain

The useful employment the Puritans envisioned for France was that of an ally with England against Spain. For although France was a Catholic power, the history of its relations with Spain seemed to the Puritans to bear resemblances to England's, and it was thought that these similarities in conjunction with contemporary political realities provided a basis for Anglo-French accord in regard to their mutual antagonist.

France, like England, was under Spanish attack, which could be shown to take the same forms as the attack on England. France, too, had felt the internal thrusts of Spanish aggression when Spain had hypocritically used religion to embroil France in civil wars. When Spain posed as the protector of Catholicism in France, it was not so much interested in religion as in a pretext to interfere in France. Spanish encouragement of civil turmoil was a means by which France

5. *Ibid.*, 89.
6. Birch, *Charles I*, I, 180–181.

was weakened and Spain gained a faction loyal to its cause. The threat was not confined to supporting internal upheavals; France had only to look about in order to comprehend how Spain and its Hapsburg relatives encircled it. The end to which the internal subversions and the external encirclement pointed was the reduction of France to the status of a Spanish dependency or, if possible, a province of Spain.[7] The fact that France was of the same religion as Spain aided rather than prevented its inclusion in the Spanish design for world dominion. This danger, revealed in recognized internal and external assaults, was shared with England and served the Puritans as a sufficient reason for France and England to maintain an alliance.

Important precedent was also marshaled to demonstrate the advisability of union with France to counter Spain. Sir John Eliot spoke of a natural alliance, but he also criticized in terms of Elizabethan precedent England's failure to remain allied with France. When Spain had sought to shatter France, Elizabeth had pacified the French, and thereby she had raised against the common foe an alliance with France and the Netherlands.[8] Here again the policies which had produced the national glories of Elizabethan England were invoked to persuade the nation that England would garner new successes by adoption of the old and proven ways. In this case the policy advocated was that France's interest with England in halting the expansion of Spanish power should be utilized to join the two countries in meeting the present critical realities.

The harmony between France and England in 1624 promised to promote actions which would validate the Elizabethan policies for this later generation, which thought that it was

7. Scott, *Newes from Pernassus*, II, 19–20, *Vox Coeli*, 19, and *The Spaniards Perpetuall Designes*.
8. Eliot, *Negotium Posterorum*, I, 35, 76–77; Cotton, *The Danger wherein the Kingdome now standeth*, 16.

faced with similar problems. Yonge reported the levying of soldiers in France for some coordinated blow against Spanish might, and Scott informed the English public of the fear felt in Spain by the expected combination of Dutch, English, and French in that military effort.[9] When the pathetic English expedition miscarried, however, and when war with Spain was followed by war with France, the useful ally was lost and the policy of Elizabeth was discarded by the government in favor of a venture that really served Spain, not England.[10] When in 1628 France did go to war against Spain, it was over conflicting claims to Mantua. Although this war accomplished the Puritan desire to see France opposed to Spain, the accomplishment was no credit to the government of Charles; according to the following observation, it was quite the contrary: "It was not any wisdom, counsel, or policy at home, that continued our peace, (for both the Kings of France and Spain had been assaulted and provoked by us,) but the mere goodness and providence of God, who turned the arms of Ammon against Gebal, and of Gebal against Ammon, that Israel might go free." [11] But in spite of the English government's unwise policy, which flew in the face of almost sacred precedent, France finally was at war with Spain; and instead of Spain's benefiting from English coldness or hostility towards France, England and the cause of true religion gained from a removal of Spanish pressure. This favorable situation was seen by an Englishman who, writing from Leghorn in 1629, expressed a wish for the long continuance of the Italian conflict because it was to England's good.[12] And in England Sir Simonds D'Ewes voiced the Puritan's happiness in 1630 at the prospect opened by the French embroiling Spain in a

9. *The Diary of Walter Yonge,* 77; Scott, *The Second Part of Vox Populi,* 3.
10. Hulme, *The Life of Sir John Eliot,* 244; Gardiner, VI, 299–310.
11. D'Ewes, I, 370.
12. *Oxinden Letters,* 50–51.

war; on these gratifying events he wrote: "The public frame of things and affairs in Christendom beyond the seas gave all God's children daily more and more cause of rejoicing and thankfulness. For the French King, Lewis the Thirteenth, still prosecuted the war in Italy and Savoy all the last summer against the Imperialists and Spaniards abroad . . ."[13]

It appeared obvious, at least to the Puritans, that England could obtain assitance for itself and the afflicted Church by using France as an ally, and it was equally apparent to them that England and those in whom England should take an interest only suffered further danger when England and France were not in concord. The several possible attitudes of England to France can be summarized in these choices: a passive France, which would permit a free rein to the Spanish enemy; a France in conflict with England, which would increase Spanish strength; a France actively joined with England in opposition to Spain, which would present a serious danger to Spain. The obvious question was how England could act sensibly on anything other than the third choice; the question was actually framed in this way:

> For who
> But unto Spaine a friend; a faithless foe
> To England good, would give advise to breake
> Our peace with France, to make our party weake,
> And force th' affronted French in league to close
> Offensive and defensive with our foes?
> Whereas the way to safeguard us, and keepe
> Proud Spaine at such a bay, she durst not peepe
> Beyond her confines, was with France to hold
> Good correspondence.[14]

Spain's friends, those subversive advocates of a policy that

13. D'Ewes, II, 1–2.
14. J. R., *The Spy,* sig. D4v.

would lead to England's conquest and religion's suppression, were to blame for England's failure to ally itself with France; for only disloyal Englishmen would seek to lead the country into a program fitted to advance Spanish designs.

In a particular sense it seemed as if Catholic France was also a kind of shibboleth by which an individual's loyalty to England and the Reformed Church could be tested. When the Palatinate, the United Provinces, or even Spain was considered, the test was applied to the individual's attitude towards the country; but when the Catholic aspect of France was considered, the policy rather than the country was the shibboleth. In this case it was not the Puritans' feelings of kinship, sympathy, or hatred that motivated their view of France; it was utility that moved them to see France as an ally against Spain. Belief in an anti-Spanish policy, which in this case was a policy to use France, was another sign by which true Protestant Englishmen were known.

The Daughter of France

"I know not how my Brother likes it, but for my part I should ever have preferred a Daughter of France to that of Spaine, and I hope the Match will not succeede, because my noble Brother Prince Charles is wise, valiant, and generous." [15] This was the heavenly advice of the late Prince Henry, upon whom the Puritans had placed so much hope in his lifetime and with whom they later unfavorably compared his father and brother. Here it was a Puritan writer who was using the dead Prince to voice a Puritan attitude; for at the period when the Spanish match appeared likely to become a fearful reality, France offered a most useful alternative. Of course, this alternative could be reasonably subsumed under the larger Puritan proposition that France was a useful ally whereas Spain, no matter the outward appearance, was

15. Scott, *Vox Coeli*, 39.

always and unalterably the hated enemy. From this proposition it followed that, as Queen of England, a Daughter of France would be preferable to an Infanta of Spain. This preference, suggested at the height of negotiations with Spain, was reiterated by other Puritans when, after the Spanish match was broken, the match between Prince Charles and Henrietta Maria was proclaimed. D'Ewes noted that "the English generally so detested the Spanish match, as they were glad of any other which freed them from the fear of that . . ." John Preston reluctantly acknowledged to Buckingham that the marriage to France was the lesser evil.[16] The French marriage, as long as the near success of the Spanish marriage was still in mind, remained popular in England; and, because it represented a shift by the government from a pro-Spanish policy, it contributed to the enthusiasm that greeted the change from Charles, Prince of Wales, to Charles I of England.[17]

To some extent Henrietta Maria had in her own right an initial popularity that was not based solely on the fact that she was not the Infanta of Spain. She was a Daughter of France, which was important to the Puritan's concept of a useful French alliance; furthermore, she was the daughter of Henri IV, which made it seem that she might even be desirable as England's Queen. For that great monarch stood very high in Puritan eyes; indeed, in the Puritan view of France he occupied something of the position reserved for Elizabeth in England. This excellent impression of Henri IV can be appreciated in Scott's last pamphlet; about one quarter of the work was devoted to the French monarch, who was extolled by Raleigh's ghost as "a Prince so absolutely excel-

16. D'Ewes, I, 257; Ball, *Life of Preston,* 108.

17. Harold Hulme, "Charles I and the Constitution," in *Conflict in Stuart England. Essays in honour of Wallace Notestein,* ed. W. A. Aiken and B. D. Henning (London, 1960), 94–95; Maclear, "Puritan Relations with Buckingham," *Huntington Library Quarterly,* 21 (February 1958), 124–125.

lent in every perfection of true honour and magnimitie, that his paralell hath not beene found in all the Historie of France . . ." [18] The greatness of Henri IV, his early Protestantism, and his continuing favor to the religious brethren all supported the wishful confidence that the virtues of the father would be reflected in the daughter who was coming over to be Queen of England.[19]

"The 21 of November, being Sunday, were divers bonfires made in London, upon notice given that the match between our Prince Charles and Henrietta, sister to the King of France, was concluded." [20] Thus Henrietta Maria received the welcome of a nation, whose joy was compounded of relief that she was not Spanish and the hopeful expectation that she might be like her father. To Sir John Eliot this French marriage was a happy omen coming before the meeting of a new Parliament; and Sir Simonds D'Ewes, who went to Whitehall to catch a glimpse of the new Queen, "perceived her to be a most absolute delicate lady, after I had exactly surveyed all the features of her face, much enlivened by her radiant and sparkling black eye. Besides, her deportment amongst her women was so sweet and humble, and her speech and looks to her other servants so mild and gracious, as I could not abstain from divers deep-fetched sighs to consider that she wanted the knowledge of the true religion." [21]

But while D'Ewes was only sighing about the lady's lack of the true religion, some of his fellow Puritans were already beginning to have second thoughts and dark suspicions about the French marriage. Walter Yonge laconically wrote: "It is said that since the Queen came into England the priests do swarm very much in London." At the time of the marriage

18. Scott, *Sir Walter Rawleighs Ghost,* 29–38 (quotation from 29).

19. Hulme, "Charles I and the Constitution," in *Conflict in Stuart England,* 94–95.

20. *The Diary of Walter Yonge,* 77; see also Gardiner, V, 274.

21. Eliot, *Negotium Posterorum,* I, 43; D'Ewes, I, 272–273.

Preston, whose good opinion Buckingham had at one time obtained, preached *The Pillar and Ground of Truth*, in which he voiced his unreconciled suspicions in the form of indirect warnings: true religion cannot be mixed with error any more than oil with water, iron with clay; Solomon in his old age turned to strange gods by his wives.[22] Further criticism was muttered in that same Parliament for which Eliot had seen the marriage as a happy prelude, but at this time the criticisms were still not directed against Henrietta Maria personally. Instead, the marriage treaty and secret concessions for the English Catholics came under attack — attack which, while avoiding the Queen, did not spare the government of her husband.[23]

The Daughter of France as Queen of England did not remain unscathed by criticism for many years. When Dyke preached before Commons in 1628, he spoke of the antediluvian world where "the Children of God, the posterity of Seth, made mongrell matches with the daughters men, the posterity of Caine." Within the year Henrietta Maria was the explicit subject of a printed attack, which stood comparison with the remarks that had previously been reserved for the Spanish Infanta. The author was Alexander Leighton, whose offensive comment merited this delightful description by a cleric: "His famed passage about his majesty's marriage (as I hear by those who have read the book) is, that 'missing an Egyptian,' meaning the Infanta, 'he had light upon a daughter of Heth,' meaning her majesty: not, as some relate, missing a Jew, had married a Turk; though it be little better, for he implies a Canaanite." [24] Nevertheless, Leighton's abuse was the exception in the period before the Civil War (which made Hen-

22. *The Diary of Walter Yonge*, 83; Preston, *Sermons Preached Before his Majestie*, 16–19, 23; Ball, *Life of Preston*, 154.

23. Birch, *Charles I*, I, 36; Eliot, *Negotium Posterorum*, II, 32–33.

24. Dyke, *A Sermon Preached at the Publicke Fast*, 3; Birch, *Charles I*, II, 62–63; Leighton, *An Appeal to the Parliament*, 172.

rietta Maria a figure of violent controversy), for it was mainly in their retrospective writings, composed long after the event, that Puritans like Lucy Hutchinson and Edmund Ludlow displayed any real animus toward the French marriage.[25]

Without a doubt there was considerable Puritan dislike of Henrietta Maria during the later upheavals in England, but the fact remains that when she first came to England she was acceptable to the Puritans. So fearful were they of the Spanish Infanta that they temporarily deluded themselves into believing that a French Princess was desirable, and only later did they doubt her desirability. Moreover, probably no Puritan, even in the depths of the Civil War, ever doubted that, if such a choice had to be made, a Daughter of France was to be preferred to a Spanish Infanta. In this way the Puritans' attitude toward the French marriage was consistent with their general attitude to Catholic France; for, although there might be little enthusiasm (the enthusiasm for Henrietta Maria was, of course, mainly a response of relief) felt for Catholic France, France was useful. As a Daughter of France had been acceptable because she was a useful alternative to something far worse, so France itself was to be tolerated because it, too, was useful as an ally against Spain. For this reason of utility the Puritans strongly urged the maintenance of the French alliance, and for the same reason they urged and for a time welcomed the French marriage.

Protestant France

To separate the Puritans' views of Catholic France from their view of Protestant France is a useful approach, but it

25. Hutchinson, *Memoirs*, I, 126; Edmund Ludlow, *The Memoirs of Edmund Ludlow*, ed. C. H. Firth (2 vols.; Oxford, 1894), I, 10.

must not be forgotten that in the political realities of the seventeenth century such a separation was not always possible. Often enough, the Puritan picture of France seems blurred, but this blurring is a natural result of the difficulties the Puritans encountered whenever they made statements about France. Such difficulties were most apparent when they found themselves poised between sympathy for the French Protestants and the necessity of urging an alliance with France against Spain when Catholic France was persecuting its Protestants. Furthermore, the Puritans had to take into account a war between England and France in which England supported the beleaguered Huguenots. The lack of precision in the Puritans' view of France is understandable, for the tension of real contradictions did not allow them the luxury of an ideal definition of a monistic attitude.

Part of their trouble was inherent, in that they clearly defined Catholic France as a useful ally against absolute evil, while they also forcefully proclaimed the Huguenots to be members of the Reformed Church and therefore fraternal participants in an absolute good. The Puritans did not doubt that a bond of true religion joined them to the French Protestants. D'Ewes confidently remarked that there was "no question made at this time, but that we and they, though differing in discipline and ceremony, made and constituted with all the other Protestants in the world, one true Catholic Church . . ." [26] It was the same spiritual kinship which Scott declared should serve to unite the Reformed Churches in spite of unimportant local differences, and whereas D'Ewes wrote privately, Scott addressed his appeal for unity to the public. John Preston, with imperiled French Protestantism foremost in his mind, delivered his appeal to the public but exclusive audience at Whitehall. In the King's presence he championed the bonds of Protestantism when he asked, "doe

26. D'Ewes, I, 164; see also Birch, *James I*, II, 123.

wee not see the whole bodie of those that professe the truth are besieged round about through Christendom . . . are not many branches of the Church cut off already, & more in hazard?"[27]

Because of the acknowledged ties of religious fellowship with the French Protestants, the Puritans could not help being moved when those brethren were subjected to persecutions. Except for the bond of Protestant marriage by a favorite Princess, the Puritan position towards the French Protestants was like their position towards the Palatinate and the persecuted of Germany. Similarly, the French Protestants offered a means of identification in England, as was evidenced by this couplet:

> A Puritan is hee which grieves to thinke
> Religion should in Fraunce, shipwrack and sincke[28]

The Religious Brethren and the Ill-advised King

The geographical nearness of England to France, furthermore, made England what it was not to the distressed of Germany, a haven for Protestant refugees from Catholic persecution. Instead of the vicarious horrors peddled by the gazeteers, the English public was confronted daily with the sight of the victims of Catholic France's intolerance. Members of Parliament did not fail to notice the French brethren who thronged Westminster Hall.[29] The Puritans, too, saw the refugees. Here to England came their coreligionists, attacked and exiled by the forces of the France which, for the good of religion and the nation, had to be the ally of England. Some, like Margaret Winthrop, emphasized the sympathetic bond and reacted to France in a direct way: "I am sorye for

27. Scott, *Digitus Dei*, 35, 37; Preston, *A sensible Demonstration of the Deity*, in *Sermons Preached Before his Majestie*, 84.

28. Scott, *The Interpreter*, 5.

29. Chamberlain, *Letters*, 382; *Commons Debates 1621*, II, 406.

the hard condishtion of Rochell. the lord helpe them and fite for them and then none shall preuayle against them or ouercome them. in vaine thay fite that fite against the lorde who is a myty god and will destroye all his enimyes . . ." [30] There were others, however, who found the problem less simple and were compelled to look more closely at the persecutor to see whether he was actually an enemy or a useful ally. When Catholic France was perceived in isolation, it was an ally; when examined in relation to Protestant France, that ally's persecutions of Protestants obviously required explanation.

The explanation usually was given in terms of the persecutor rather than the victims, and it exposed an interesting Puritan attitude towards Louis XIII. Louis himself was viewed as a victim — not of persecution, to be sure, but of Spanish deceptions and pro-Spanish subversions. To some extent, then, the French Protestants were not suffering at the hands of Catholic France; instead, they suffered because of the machinations of Spain, that perfect embodiment of evil.

One Puritan claim was that Spain tricked France into attacking the Huguenots in order that Spain might use the opportunity to seize the Valtelline and thereby disadvantage a distracted France.[31] More often, though, the Puritans charged that Louis was misled by advisers who owed a Spanish allegiance, and it was upon these "Hispaniolized counsellors" that the blame for the persecutions was placed.[32] Thus, the burden of guilt weighed lightly on the King of France, while it rested heavily on the real enemy of both France and England.

Nor did the Puritans neglect to mention an outcome of the French King's ill-advised persecution of his Protestant subjects. Scott in almost scriptural language gave this descrip-

30. *Winthrop Papers*, ed. S. E. Morison et al. (5 vols.; Boston, 1929–1947), II, 59.

31. Scott, *Votivae Angliae*, sig. B4.

32. *The Diary of Walter Yonge*, 48; Scott, *The Interpreter*, 5; D'Ewes, I, 164.

tion: "what did those attemps beget but the faire birth of increase of religion, and firme opposition against un-princely cruelty, and unnaturall enforcement? and he went away affrighted at his owne handiworke, and cursing the mo-tives and setters on of his presumption: which abated his malice, and taught him to know there was a God above princes . . ."[33] Moreover, after Louis XIII was made aware of the hazard to France of the subversive advice of disloyal councillors, he discovered through Richelieu's guidance the value of his truly loyal Protestant subjects.[34]

In all this tender cultivation of the French King, even when that monarch was unhelpfully attacking the religious brethren, the Puritans seemed to keep in mind the impor-tance of France as an ally against Spain. Their method was to absolve Louis XIII of wrongdoing by claiming that his ac-tions were the result of Spanish deceptions. This explanation of the French King's relationship to the French Protestants has some parallels in the Puritan examination of James I's conduct towards the Protestants in Germany. In both in-stances the monarchs were portrayed as either duped by Spain or misled by pro-Spanish councillors. But whereas gullibility was the worst accusation brought against Louis XIII, James I suffered considerably harsher criticism. More was to be expected from James, of course, but it cannot be denied that the English Puritans were extremely careful to cast the most favorable light on the ruler of the useful ally.

French War and English Reactions

Forbearance from criticism of Louis XIII constituted an attempt to maintain the utility of France, but it did not constitute Puritan approval of the King's persecutions. No matter that the true source of Huguenot sufferings lay with

33. Scott, *The Belgick Souldier*, 28.
34. Birch, *Charles I*, II, 179.

Spain; the fact remained, as the flow of refugees testified, that members of the Reformed Church were suffering in France. They could not be ignored; there had to be succour for them. The same sense of unity that compelled the Puritans to speak out for the Palatinate motivated their appeals for England's assistance to the French brethren. For the Puritans, intervention in favor of the Protestant cause had to be England's policy, and that cause was endangered in France by the ill-advised assault of Louis XIII on La Rochelle.[35]

The question of English intervention was a religious one for the Puritans; but when England did intervene, was it for religious reasons? Certainly the government of King Charles wanted it to appear that there was a religious reason for war with France. Secretary Conway directed Laud, then Bishop of London, to prepare a public prayer to be used in the services throughout his diocese; and Conway added: "He will not omit in this prayer the religious end of this expedition, to give relief to an oppressed church, and support to the profession of true religion."[36] The government clearly wanted England to believe that the motive for the war was to serve the Protestant cause abroad. Later, however, when Edmund Ludlow, the Puritan military commander and republican leader, recalled the French war from his exile in Switzerland, he felt that Charles's resolution had had quite a different origin. He stated: "The King having assumed this extraordinary power, resolved to make war against France, not upon the account of those of the reformed religion, as was pretended, but grounded upon personal discontents, and to gratify the revenge and lust of his favourite."[37] From the standpoint of Edmund Ludlow, what the King did to aid La Rochelle might have been right, but the reason was wrong.

35. Hill, *Puritanism and Revolution*, 251–253; Preston, *A sensible Demonstration of the Deity*, in *Sermons Preached Before his Majestie*, 84.

36. PRO SP 16/113/52.

37. Ludlow, *Memoirs*, I, 11.

An English relief expedition was mounted under the leadership of the Duke of Buckingham, whose position as favorite and whose personal courage in the field were insufficient qualities to compensate for his lack of any other worthwhile ability. When the fleet departed England, a letter writer expressed no optimism either for its success or for any good it would do for the French Protestants. This melancholy prediction was remarkably verified by events: "The flower of our soldiery, both for land and sea, are now there; and, if they return in vain, how vain shall we be esteemed? In the meantime, the danger of the Protestants there must be as great as that king's jealousy, by reason of the approach of our forces." [38]

Ill-planned and ill-led, the English attempt to save the citadel of the French Protestants was a military disaster that produced a feeling of national disaster in England. Although in the years 1618 to 1640 no completely English military force tasted a real victory, the defeat at Ré was the largest and most humiliating of the failures. The English Puritans, in trying to comprehend the failure, sought for its cause within England, where they discovered not simple miscalculation or weakness but betrayal. False Englishmen had led England to defeat and thereby had led England to betray the French Protestants.

This betrayal had, in fact, a prelude, which in its own time had been denounced as dangerous to the religious brethren. The earlier betrayal was seen in the loan of English ships by Charles to his French brother-in-law in 1625, when Louis was already engaged against his Protestant subjects. The English sailors, however, refused to serve where they might be called upon to shed Protestant blood, and in 1625 and 1626 the loan was questioned in Parliament and condemned from the pulpit.[39] Years later when two Puritans, Lucy Hutchinson

38. Birch, *Charles I,* I, 250.
39. PRO SP 16/4/40 and SP 16/23/30.

and Edmund Ludlow, wrote of this, they both displayed the affair as an example of the English government's policy to ruin religion abroad because, in Lucy Hutchinson's words, "the protestants abroad were all looked upon as Puritans . . ." [40]

When England was required to assist the besieged La Rochelle, the hesitancy with which the government approached its solemn obligations provoked some fears that the Huguenots might be left to perish. In retrospect it seemed that the Rochellers would have been better off without England's aid; for the English forces at Ré, instead of raising the French siege, weakened Rochelle's defense by requiring already scarce provisions from the town. "It may justly be said of us, & them," Leighton bitterly wrote, "as it was said of Israels waiting, for such help as deceived them, 'their eyes failed for our vain help; in our watching we have watched for a nation that could not save.' " Such a weakening was not viewed as an accident or an error in supply; it was later looked upon as part of a calculated plan of disservice to England and ruin to the French Protestants. Here is Mrs. Hutchinson's description and opinion on the failure of an expedition begun with such reluctance: "all the flower of the English gentry were lost in an ill-managed expedition to the Isle of Rhe, under pretence of helping them, but so ordered that it proved the loss of Rochelle, the strong fort and best defence of all the protestants in France." [41]

After La Rochelle surrendered to its sovereign, there continued in England the search for those who had perverted the English effort into defeat for England and ruin for the French Protestants. The individual most susceptible to blame was not Charles, who was shielded from immediate responsibility for the betrayal, but his favorite and factotum, the

40. Hutchinson, *Memoirs*, I, 122. See also, Ludlow, *Memoirs*, I, 11–12.

41. Birch, *Charles I*, I, 380; Ludlow, *Memoirs*, I, 11–12; Leighton, *An Appeal to the Parliament*, 269; Hutchinson, *Memoirs*, I, 122.

Duke of Buckingham. To a large extent Buckingham could not avoid responsibility, for he was without question the King's chief adviser and the actual field commander at Ré. Vigorous, even bitter, criticism was therefore aimed at Buckingham. D'Ewes said that the expedition itself had been wrong because England would have been more effective, or at least would not have damaged the efforts of the Rochellers, had it chosen to assist Denmark. Moreover, Buckingham was denounced for having had false motives in wanting the war with France. It was not for the sake of embattled religion that he had sent Englishmen to die; it was the spurning of his immoral lusts that was said to have provoked him to this war.[42] Buckingham had planned the wrong expedition for the wrong reasons; but, for whatever reason the task was undertaken, he was the wrong man to command. One author addressed the fallen town with the statement that it would have been saved

> Had we, in thy defence, imploy'd that host,
> Commanded by some one, well knowne to be
> Faithful, and of well try'd sufficiency.[43]

And the following welcome to the Duke was probably more in accord with popular feeling than the triumphal salute Charles offered:

> Art thou return'd againe, with all thy faults,
> Thou great Commander of the All-goe-naughts!
>
> .   .   .   .   .
>
> Three things have lost our honour, men surmise;
> Thy treachery, neglect, and cowardise.[44]

It seemed to some Englishmen that Buckingham's only ac-

42. J. R., *The Spy*, sigs. E1v–E3v; D'Ewes, I, 364–365, 393–399; Ludlow, *Memoirs*, I, 11

43. J. R., *The Spy*, sig. E3.

44. PRO SP 16/85/84. John Rous copied the verses into his diary (see *Diary*, 19–22).

complishment was to have ruined the cause of the Reformed Church, and his only ability was to make enemies.[45] Finally one Englishman, acting upon an offense received from the Duke and upon the public outcry at his deeds, murdered Buckingham.[46] John Felton made an end to this enemy to England and betrayer of Protestantism; but, unfortunately for Charles, Buckingham's death did not really lay to rest the discontents that had focused upon the late Duke. The disgrace England had suffered did not die with its promoter.

No other single occurrence of this period aroused such an intense feeling of national dishonor as that which gripped England after the retreat from Ré and the capitulation of La Rochelle. There was a certain justice in a letter of appeal to England from the besieged town which predicted that God would require of England their blood; but the blood requirement took the form of shame for honor lost by betrayal.[47] Also from outside England came the victor's scorn to reinforce the bitterness of defeat, to bruise the wounded pride.[48] England was shamed before the world.

Within England that wound went deep. One writer revealed his feelings when he described the defeat as "the greatest and shamefullest overthrow the English have received since we lost Normandy . . ." D'Ewes, coming to London, observed the public reaction and reported that he "saw sadness and dejectedness almost in every man's face . . ." The sense of dishonor knew no confines, for even one so definitely non-Puritan as John Evelyn remembered those sad times and referred to "our disgrace before La Rochelle." [49] The wound was very deep indeed.

45. Leighton, *An Appeal to the Parliament*, 211, 269.
46. *CSPD, Charles I*, III, 271, 310; Clarendon, *History*, I, 33–34. See also the bitter epitaph in Rous, *Diary*, 29–30.
47. Birch, *Charles I*, I, 380.
48. *Ibid.*, 281; Leighton, *An Appeal to the Parliament*, 270.
49. Birch, *Charles I*, I, 285; D'Ewes, I, 361; *The Diary of John Evelyn*, ed. E. S. de Beer (6 vols.; Oxford, 1955), II, 8–9.

Nevertheless, as in the case of most events abroad, the dishonorable defeat did not exist in isolation from matters within England. The actual loss had been used to attack Buckingham as all-powerful chief minister, and similarly the laments about England's consequent loss of honor were often inseparable from criticisms of the serious condition of England. An Englishman, writing from Leyden, demonstrated how the reflection of external events upon internal faults was joined in a single thought: "I am sorrye for our overthrow at Isle of Reyes, that is all the talk now here and of the desperate disease of our Commonwealth at home." D'Ewes, too, combined the criticisms when in a single sentence he remarked on the sadness following defeat and the royal pressures to collect a forced loan. This combination of complaints was echoed in Commons, where Sir John Eliot, the leading parliamentary figure of 1629, voiced the dejection of Englishmen about "all our late actions forreign or domesticke" which had lost "our reputation, our honor." [50]

This feeling of disgrace, which fused foreign disaster with domestic discontents, outlived Buckingham, who had served as a political lightning rod for the criticisms against the monarch. When he was gone, Charles was left without the friend, which loss he lamented; and the King was left without the shield, which loss he might have more profitably regretted. In 1628 John Vicars, then the unruly Puritan minister of Stamford, was alleged to have prayed God to make Charles rejoice in the death of Buckingham, "that wicked Achan." [51] By 1629 the King, who until then had not been blamed for the betrayal and dishonor, was condemned in two libels for the fate of La Rochelle and for the breaking of Parliament, for which reasons, the libels pronounced, Charles had lost the hearts of his people and the protection of God, and would

50. *Oxinden Letters*, 33; D'Ewes, I, 361; Eliot, *Negotium Posterorum*, II, 134–135.
51. PRO SP 16/119/52.

lose his throne in the manner of a Saul or a Balthazar.[52] In this way the sufferings of a part of the Reformed Church were mixed with the domestic situation in England to become not just a demand concerning foreign policy but a whip to chastise the makers of policy for their part in the calamities religion suffered.

An Approach to the Puritan Attitude to France

The Puritan picture of two Frances could not, of course, be totally consistent, but neither was it totally contradictory. There was difficulty in viewing Catholic France as a useful ally, which had to be encouraged by England, while simultaneously viewing a faction within that ally as religious brethren, whose cause had to be England's. Still, this difficulty was indicative of a larger consistency in the Puritans' thinking, for their consistent belief was that Protestantism always had to be defended against its most important enemy — Spain. France, even more than the Netherlands, was imperfect; but because it also was threatened by Spain it was seen to have a common cause with England and the Protestant nations. Nevertheless, the utility of France did not, in the Puritan view, permit England to ignore the persecution of the French Protestants. The protection of Protestantism was paramount, and England's intervention would have been the correct act if only it had been successful. Instead, England betrayed the French Protestants, who were forced to surrender, and England obviously alienated Catholic France as an ally. By this double failure England lost for Protestantism much of the strength of an important member of that body and lost for a time all the strength of a useful ally against Protestantism's greatest danger. Because of England's folly, which appeared

52. PRO SP 16/142/92, 93.

to the Puritans as treachery calculated to destroy Protestantism, their overriding policy was doubly damaged without any compensatory benefit to religion or England.

It is little wonder, then, that these failures by the English government, following the failure to secure the other suffering members of the Church in the Palatinate, provoked a bitter reaction in England, reaction that does not seem to have been confined to the Puritans alone. The English government previously had failed to prevent defeats to Protestantism, and for that it had been criticized sharply; but the government of Charles I had done worse: it had actually contributed to a disaster to Protestantism. The Puritans held that England's only true interests were those of a nation devoted to the cause of God; they could not long hold with a government that had helped to suppress God's Church in France and to endanger it everywhere.

VI

The King of Sweden

Then, as now, the figure of Gustavus Adolphus stood as a giant among men in the history of the Thirty Years' War. His career was brief at the center of the European stage, but the brevity only served to heighten his stature and enlarge his legend. In the darkest hour he came, brought light, and departed; when he was gone, the bright light of victory was dimmed but not snuffed out. If, after Gustavus Adolphus, Protestantism did not triumph, neither did it collapse. He had saved it.[1]

1. C. V. Wedgwood, *The Thirty Years War* (London, 1957), 204–348 *passim;* this part of Miss Wedgwood's history was especially helpful for its clear exposition of the career of Gustavus Adolphus and the events in Europe from 1628 to 1635. The sources for the English reactions to the King of Sweden and the affairs of Europe in the early 1630's are meager, probably because of the tighter government controls over press and pulpit, the loss of Parliament as a forum of public expression, and the deaths of Thomas Scott, the zealous pamphleteer, and John Chamberlain, the observant correspondent.

The Time of Despair

In England, where the Puritans anxiously watched the uncertain course of Protestantism in Europe, the King of Sweden came to occupy a unique position: he was an embodiment of near perfection. Among the nations only Spain was perfect, but that was perfect evil. The other nations, even the Protestant nations, had good and evil qualities mixed, and therefore they could not be wholly admirable. Sweden, however, was not given much consideration as a nation. It was viewed, instead, in the person of its King, who was seen as the peerless warrior of the Church, the nearly faultless man, an ideal. Hence, it was not to the country of Sweden that the Puritans responded, it was to the King of Sweden; and their response to the King was not so much a response to the man as to a Protestant ideal that was acting in the world.

Nevertheless, without in any way detracting from the immediate importance of the Swedish actions, the response in England to those actions must be appraised in terms of the moment. For in order to measure the contemporary significance of the Swedish victories, it should be remembered that they came when the Protestant position in Germany was at its nadir. As great as the King of Sweden's triumphs were, they appeared even larger in the context of their initial occurrence. It was an explosive dawn ending a dismal night.

In England expectations were also low. After the enthusiasms that greet any new monarch, the first five years under King Charles offered the English Puritans few reasons for satisfaction about their country. In foreign affairs England had staggered from weakness to betrayal, from failure to defeat, and Protestantism seemed only to have lost by everything England did. Nor could the Puritans take any comfort in the course of domestic affairs. By 1630 Parliament, in which the Puritans placed much hope, was unlikely to be summoned again; and at least one preacher's sorrowful remarks on the breaking of Parliament were followed by sympathetic comments on the plans for a New England.[2] In the Church, Laud, though not in fact Archbishop, was already exercising the powers of an Archbishop of Canterbury with an influence that went far beyond the affairs of the Anglican Church. During these years there were for England only two events in which the Puritans could see any merit; yet neither the failure of the Spanish Infanta to become Queen of England nor the death of the Duke of Buckingham could be construed as a positive accomplishment for England and the true religion. Indeed, in 1630 the Puritans could not see England doing anything to cure itself; such an England could perform nothing for the religious brethren abroad, who appeared prostrate, in momentary expectation of a death blow.

However bad matters were for England, it was not confronted with the likelihood of imminent destruction that faced European Protestantism in 1630. In France the Huguenots had lost their great fortress of La Rochelle, and they were at the mercy of their sovereign. But it was in Germany, where the war had begun, that the danger was greatest, for there the Protestants were not faced with a monarch like the reasonably lenient Louis XIII. Instead, they had to contend with Hapsburgs: the Emperor Ferdinand II and his Spanish cousins. Moreover, by 1630 the Protestants were virtually defenceless, while the Emperor had gone from strength to strength. Denmark, the latest nation to enter the lists in defense of the Reformed, was decisively beaten by Wallenstein, and that commander was assigned by the Emperor to enforce the Edict of Restitution, restoring to the Roman Church all the property it had lost since 1555. With the

2. PRO SP 16/142/94.

passing of more than a decade of bloody warfare, there was the prospect in 1630 that the war would soon end; but the way it would have ended then was a most unhappy prospect for Protestantism.

Religion's peril did not go unnoticed in England, where the deepening domestic crisis kept in step with feelings of despair for the afflicted Church across the sea. D'Ewes devoted several pages to reciting and lamenting all the disasters that had befallen "the cause of God's church and children" just in the year 1626.[3] He, along with many other Englishmen, would have concurred in this estimation of the comparative political and military strength of Protestantism and its persecuting enemies: "So that comparing our weaknesse, with their strength; their skilfulness, with our unaptnesse; their readinesse, with our want of experience; their sedulity, with our securitie; our danger is great: we have no better refuge, then to fly to the mercy & protection of the Almighty, who hath hitherto mightily defended us. Arise therefore, O Lord God of Hosts, maintaine thine owne cause, and fight for us . . ."[4] Still, the longed-for salvation of Protestantism from its calamitous situation did not arrive swiftly. Before the King of Sweden could win a single battle against the Catholic forces, the Protestants suffered the terrible loss of Magdeburg in a fury of fire and slaughter. In England that fearful destruction evoked horrified reaction.[5] The fortunes of the religious brethren had fallen to their lowest point, and some Englishmen despaired of their brethren's fate. So great was the Church's peril by 1630 that Richard Sibbes transmuted profound despair into ultimate hope when he promised that "Christ and his Church when they are at the lowest, are

3. D'Ewes, I, 347–349.
4. Hampton, *A Proclamation of Warre*, 23.
5. *Fairfax Correspondence*, I, 234.

neerest rising: his enemies at the highest are neerest a downe-fall." [6]

The Warrior of the Church

The contrast between the dark peril of Protestantism and the sudden alteration in its favor made the victories of Gustavus Adolphus seem even more glorious than they were. Despair changed to triumph. In England the intensity of the interest in the dramatic reversal in Germany can be gauged by the avidness with which the English public sought for every scrap of news about the Swedish hero and his victories for religion. In 1632 England was deluged with books about Sweden and the military campaigns of Gustavus Adolphus. The first four parts of *The Swedish Intelligencer,* amounting to about 900 pages, were published in four editions that year, and there were also such works as *The Swedish Discipline* and *The Swedish Devotions* to meet the demands of the public for news of the King of Sweden.[7] Englishmen not only eagerly read and heard of the events in Germany, but they demonstrated that their interest was more than transient by taking the trouble to record the latest news.[8]

As enormous as the output of news pamphlets and as great as the public interest were, it was not surprising that publisher and public were too often gullible about any item concerning the Swedish venture. Sir John Eliot, although a

6. Richard Sibbes, *The Bruised Reede, and Smoaking Flax* (London, 1630), 339–340. See also Taylor, *Christs Victorie over the Dragon,* 325–326, 721–722, 817–818.

7. These titles are only a small sample from 1632 of the news reports of the Swedish campaign; the succeeding years were equally productive in the output of printed materials about Gustavus Adolphus. See *STC* and Joseph Frank, *The Beginnings of the English Newspaper 1620–1660* (Cambridge, Mass., 1961), 14–15, 301 n. 70.

8. D'Ewes, II, 57–64, 83–86.

prisoner in the Tower, had easy access to the latest reports from abroad, but he held belief in check until he could obtain confirmation on some reports of a great Swedish victory.[9] The eagerness that inspired a too-ready public acceptance of any rumor led a preacher at Oxford to pray the "curranto-makers" might know the spirit of truth in order that the public could know when to offer praises for the King of Sweden's victories and when to offer prayers for him in his distresses.[10]

The volume of news received and recorded about the Swedish invasion indicated a large English interest, an interest not confined to any particular group of Englishmen. Nevertheless, the size of the English interest was only one aspect of the enthusiastic response created by the victories of Gustavus Adolphus. Enthusiasm was revealed in the exclamatory manner in which individuals reported or commented on the latest information.[11] Enthusiasm was further displayed in the care taken to credit the triumphs to the Swedes, almost to the exclusion of all others.[12] Although the interest was general and the response widespread, the extreme forms of that response came from Puritans. John Workman, preacher at Gloucester, was cited before the High Commission for a long list of strongly nonconformist opinions, including his action in offering prayer for Gustavus Adolphus before praying for King Charles.[13] A less public but even more remarkable kind of enthusiasm was the deeply personal meaning the victories had for D'Ewes. He found such great joy in the Swedish

9. Sir John Eliot, *The Letter-Book of Sir John Eliot, 1625–1632,* ed. A. B. Grosart (2 vols.; London, 1882), II, 200–201.

10. PRO SP 16/224/47. A Star Chamber decree a week earlier ordered the suppression of the news gazettes, and the decree specifically cited the two most prominent booksellers, Nathaniel Butter and Nicholas Bourne. The prohibition did not remain in effect for long, and the gazeteers were soon in business again. *CSPD, Charles I,* V, 426, VI, 222.

11. Eliot, *The Letter-Book,* II, 200–201; PRO SP 16/222/37.

12. D'Ewes II, 3.

13. PRO SP 16/261/F, 206v–207.

King's war for Protestantism that he feared his joy made him prideful, for which he thought he was punished by God. He described his fault and punishment: "But now the glorious King of Sweden's victories having given us comfort abroad, (of which I would often say I was more sensible and joyful than of the birth of a son,) and my father's decease having brought me wealth and plenty . . . I had been in greater danger of the sin of pride and a haughty mind, had not my good God by this vast loss of my dearest child, and by other afflictions, much cast me down." [14] When victory reversed despair, the joyous response to the Swedish successes became intense and very personal.

Enthusiasm was the most prominent English reaction, but it was not the sole reaction. The victories over the Catholic forces also inspired feelings of satisfaction that the afflictions suffered by the religious brethren were now being rightly avenged. Specifically, the decisive defeat of Tilly near Leipzig was seen as vengeance upon him for the inhuman performance of his army at Magdeburg.[15] Generally, the Swedish conquests were a retribution for the years of Protestant sufferings; they were "God's just scourge . . . to avenge him on the bloody and lustful soldiers of the Emperor's army, to abate their pride . . ." [16] And in England there was a complementary response in the English hopes for the continued triumphs of Swedish arms, fighting for the once nearly hopeless cause of the Church in Germany, destroying the implacable enemies to true religion.[17] The King of Sweden had lifted Protestantism from catastrophe to victory, while in England the political alteration was matched by a change from hopelessness to expectation.

The interest and enthusiasm with which England responded

14. D'Ewes, II, 46–47.
15. *Ibid.*, 64.
16. *Ibid.*, 84 (source of quotation); Gouge, *The Saints Sacrifice*, 289–290.
17. *Fairfax Correspondence*, I, 254; PRO SP 16/214/76.

to the Swedish attack against the Hapsburgs was, in large part, an expression of gladness for the rescue of religion in Germany. Gustavus Adolphus was the military savior of the afflicted Church, and in that role of warrior of the Church he had a special relationship to God. William Gouge saluted him as "Deliverer," "Defender of the true religion," "another Cyrus, the Lords Annointed, whose right hand the Lord hath holden to subdue nations before him." [18] He was both servant and favorite: as he served the Church by redeeming it from bondage and persecution, he was marked by divine favor.

Prior to his invasion of the Empire the King of Sweden had displayed his devotion to religion by inviting "all the distressed Protestants in Germany to repair unto his kingdom with their wives and families, and there to inhabit." [19] The invitation of 1628 was noted as one sign of his attachment to the cause of the Church, but it paled before his great deeds of 1631 and 1632, deeds which Englishmen claimed were battles that Gustavus Adolphus fought for God.[20] Thus, this monarch appeared to the English as the Protestant warrior, serving God by saving the temporal Church from its antichristian enemies.

The English also observed the way Gustavus Adolphus rendered further service to God by his personal religious practice. One of the news tracts gave considerable space to the religiosity of that monarch, comparing him to Joshua and printing some of the prayers he offered in times of great danger.[21] When the danger was past and victory won, the

18. Gouge, *The Saints Sacrifice*, 284.
19. D'Ewes, I, 398.
20. PRO SP 16/224/47; Gouge, *The Saints Sacrifice*, 292.
21. *The Swedish Discipline, Religious, Civile, And Military. The First Pare, in the Formes of Prayer daily used by those of the Swedish Nation, in the Armie. Together with two severall Prayers, uttered upon severall occasions by that pious King, which God immediately heard and granted him* (London, 1632), 4–35.

Swedish King was said to give the sole glory to God in acknowledgement of divine assistance in all his successes.[22] Here was a King who actively served the Church, who was glorious in that service, but who, instead of reserving the glory for himself, rendered it to God, for whom he battled. Here was a King for the English to admire, and admire they did. So much was he admired that a fault in him was easily turned into a virtue; when D'Ewes came to write of the pride in victory which overtook Gustavus Adolphus, the devout Puritan mentioned the sin only as a possibility and thought that the weakness was not the King's as much as it was the fault of those men who "looked too much upon the arm of flesh in him." [23] There was no desire to blemish the picture of this royal servant, working humbly and gratefully in God's service.

Englishmen saw this King of Sweden devoting himself to the needs of the Church, and they saw God rewarding this servant with large favors. Initially, God was said to have selected Gustavus Adolphus to be a scourge to the oppressors of the Church.[24] Having chosen him to smite the legions of Antichrist, God then sustained the King when he prayed for divine help in his hazardous undertakings.[25] Those demonstrations of God's favor to Gustavus Adolphus were understood by some Englishmen to mean that God was rescuing the

22. D'Ewes, II, 59.

23. *Ibid.*, 85. The report of this purported fault in Gustavus Adolphus came to D'Ewes indirectly from the Scottish minister to whom the King had confessed the matter. Thus, even the means by which the weakness was revealed showed the King of Sweden to be a humble and contrite man, and possible criticism really became another type of praise for his devotion to religion. It is also worthwhile to note that the antipathy D'Ewes had demonstrated towards Lutherans in no way affected his unqualified admiration of the Lutheran King of Sweden; however, he still had no respect for the attitudes of the other Protestant German Princes. See D'Ewes, I, 259, II, 3.

24. *Ibid.*, 84; Gouge, *The Saints Sacrifice*, 289-290.

25. *The Swedish Discipline*, 29-35.

professors of true religion through the agency of the Swedish King. From his Tower cell Sir John Eliot gave testimony of his belief: "ther is enough even of miracle besides it; both for our praise and wonder; the successes both of Sweden and the States, shew him that is invisible; & by those workes he has an influence over us, of wch some signes are pregnant." [26] Confident of his divine calling and divine protection, men reasonably expected future triumphs for this instrument of God.[27] In serving God the King of Sweden had been favored by God to lift the broken body of the Church in Germany and to restore it triumphally; now with victory appearing more glorious in comparison with the despair that had reigned such a short time before, it was only natural that interested Englishmen should expect more news of great Protestant victories won by the all-conquering King of Sweden. A leading Puritan minister expressed his hopeful expectations in a prayer for Gustavus Adolphus: "And now good Lord, as thou has given such occasions of praising thy name, perfect this praise by perfecting the good work which thou hast begun for thy Churches. Leave not him whom thou has raised up to be thy Churches Deliverer, to the malitious and mischievous plots of his enemies. Be thou his strength, his rocke, his fortresse, his Deliverer. Uphold him with thy right hand, till he have performed all thy pleasure. Amen. Amen." [28]

Disbelief, Despair, and Discontent

In the darkness of 16 November 1632 soldiers searching the battlefield of Lutzen found the corpse of Gustavus Adolphus. He had won his last victory.

26. Eliot, *The Letter-Book*, II, 195. See also PRO SP 16/214/76.
27. *Fairfax Correspondence*, I, 254.
28. Gouge, *The Saints Sacrifice*, 294.

In England there was small consolation in the knowledge that the King of Sweden had died while delivering another great blow for Protestantism. Where men had been credulous in accepting unreliable news of previous triumphs, there was now no eagerness to believe the first reports of the Swedish King's death. John Bradshaw, later president of the regicide tribunal, seemed to want to find a reason for disbelief when he wrote, "God grant that the next intelligence Confirme or better this, ffor more sad or Heavie Tydings hath not in this Age bene brought since Prince Harrie's Death to the true Hearted English." [29] When the information proved true, D'Ewes, who had closely followed the King's spectacular career, wrote of his feelings and those of many others: "Never did one person's death in Christendom bring so much sorrow to all true Protestant hearts . . . as did the King of Sweden's at this present, although the affairs of Germany stood yet in as good condition as whilst the King lived." [30]

Although the death came in victory, the lamentations were not misplaced; for the newly won condition of religion in Germany could not be assured without the presence of Gustavus Adolphus himself. Even while D'Ewes saw German affairs still favorable, at least one Englishman was more prescient, fearing that without the King there would be a deterioration in the alliances he had enforced among the Protestant rulers in the Empire.[31] That prediction was realized when on 6 September 1634 the Protestant army, now commanded by a Swede and a German, suffered a total defeat at the hands of the young Hapsburg cousins. D'Ewes succinctly compre-

29. Lady Newton, *The House of Lyme* (London, 1917), 135. Contrary to Lady Newton's opinion, this letter, judging by its date and contents, seems to be about Gustavus Adolphus rather than the Elector Palatine, who died of plague, not in battle. See Hill, *Puritanism and Revolution*, 129, where Gustavus Adolphus is accepted as the subject of the letter.

30. D'Ewes, II, 86. See also the poem of lamentation Rous composed (*Diary*, 73–75).

31. Birch, *Charles I*, II, 201.

hended what had been lost in that battle: "For, as touching the present state of desolate Germany, all the victories the glorious King of Sweden had acquired in two years and some odd months whilst he lived, and all the good successes his armies had gleaned up since his decease, were all dashed at one blow, and as it were unravelled by the fatal and never-enough-to-be-lamented defeat of the Protestant army near Nordlingen . . ." [32] There had been good reason to bewail the loss of Gustavus Adolphus, for now it seemed to Englishmen that without him the cause of religion in Germany was again to be lost.[33]

The hopes that had been built upon the successes of the King of Sweden did not die easily. It is indicative, in fact, of the real depression of Protestant hopes that some men refused to give up their unrealistic hopes. In 1633 and 1634 Secretary Coke was addressed by a visionary who asserted that Gustavus Adolphus was alive in "Seleutia" and would come again to fight against Rome, or (in a later account) that he would come out of a prison and be first recognized by his daughter.[34] Such illusions sprang from dashed hopes; in clearer minds, where lingering hope was no longer compatible with reality, there was a reversion to the despair for Protestantism that had preceded the advent of Gustavus Adolphus to save the Church in Germany.[35] Now there reappeared the desperate, ultimate optimism which promised that the lowest ebb marked the nearness of restoration, victory, and glory.[36] As a matter of fact, even after Nordlingen the posi-

32. D'Ewes, II, 110–111.
33. Gardiner, VII, 372–373.
34. PRO SP 16/246/19, SP 16/277/5.
35. PRO SP 16/297/39.
36. John Goodwin, *The Saints interest in God; opened in severall sermons, preached Anniversarily upon the fifth of November* (London, 1640), 215–256, 269–272. Goodwin preached these sermons in 1633–34; the published version was dedicated to Isaac Pennington and Goodwin's other parishioners at St. Stephens, Coleman Street.

tion of Protestantism was not reduced to its former jeopardy, but neither was the position as favorable as it had been when Gustavus Adolphus lived and fought. Contemporaries could not be expected to know the course of a war which was not yet at its halfway point when the warrior of the Church was slain. What they saw was defeat turned to victory and re-turned to defeat, and in light of those alternations in fortune the feelings in England are understandable.

A return to despair was not the only English response to the King of Sweden's death and the defeat of the Protestant army at Nordlingen. Englishmen were not content to look solely at the unhappy condition of their religious brethren in Germany; they also looked at England and at what England had done for Gustavus Adolphus and those for whom he had fought and died. Inquiry along these lines reflected on the government of England. The reflection was not good.

It cannot be said that the English government was not forewarned as to the wisdom of actively supporting Gustavus Adolphus. Sir Thomas Roe, probably the most experienced English diplomat of the period, advised Charles through the Earl of Holland concerning England's relations with the King of Sweden. Sir Thomas urged that England assist with money and, more important, "by countenance and reputation of unity" so that Gustavus Adolphus would be assured of his Protestant allies.[37] Protestant unity, however, had never been part of the foreign policy of Charles, and the importance placed upon it by Roe was not likely to be heeded by his sovereign.

Neither was there any likelihood of financial support from England; Charles, having resolved to be rid of Parliaments, was in no position to finance anyone's ventures. Yet, for those Englishmen most concerned about the fate of Protestantism, this reason for the lack of funds with which to supply the

37. *CSPD, Charles I,* V, 401.

warrior of the Church could in no way excuse England's King. To the contrary, the necessities of the religious brethren were but another argument for not dispensing with Parliament. Thus, those Englishmen firmest for religion were also firmest for a Parliament from which aid for Gustavus Adolphus — or, later, his successors — might have been obtained.[38] Here, again, was an instance of the nexus between the condition of religion abroad and the condition of affairs in England. Here, too, the adverse reflection was upon Charles and his government — now a personal government deprived of Buckingham's presence to deflect discontent from the King's person.

Although only visible by implication, the discontent of Englishmen over their nation's failure to maintain the Swedish campaign did touch the person of Charles I. Two Puritans, Bradshaw and D'Ewes, displayed a profound sense of Protestantism's loss in the death of Gustavus Adolphus, and in their expressions of lamentation they both compared that King's death with, to use D'Ewes' words, the death of "our late heroic and inestimable Prince Henry."[39] The setback religion suffered by the untimely removal of Gustavus Adolphus from the German battleground was equated with the mishap Protestantism had sustained when the youthful Prince Henry died, leaving his younger brother to become Prince of Wales and then Charles I. This King who would do nothing good for the afflicted brethren might otherwise never have reigned, and England would have had a sovereign to rival Gustavus Adolphus in performing wonders for religion and also for England.

Apart from that note of implied repudiation of Charles and a sense of more intensely personal involvement, no significant distinction can be made between the Puritan view of

38. *Fairfax Correspondence,* II, 261–262; PRO SP 16/232/52.
39. D'Ewes, II, 86; Newton, *House of Lyme,* 135.

the King of Sweden and the opinions held by an articulate English public. Perhaps this similarity arose from different motivations: the Puritans' position was a consistent segment of their concern for Protestantism everywhere, while the public's attitude was influenced by the attractive spectacle of a Protestant hero. What motivated the public is not important here; the important point is that English public opinion and English Puritan opinion concurred in holding an exalted view of Gustavus Adolphus. He was the personification of the ideal of a Protestant monarch: chosen by God, he warred to rescue the Church from the assaults of the legions of Antichrist. In contrast with this English picture of the ideal ruler stood the record of England's ruler, and it was this record of failure that was now repudiated by the English Puritans and the public, opposing in their common view the policies of Charles I.

VII

The Mirror of England

Although in the Puritan views of foreign nations there were several recurrent themes, one consistent impulse gave force to the Puritans' attitudes: a concern for the true religion. The Church, by which they meant the Reformed Churches, was visible in different forms in different nations; but those religious bodies were essentially parts of the same Church. England, too, was a fragment of that Church which had other fragments in other countries. For the sake of the Church the Puritans held that England had to be interested in the scattered religious brethren, and it was this concern that was at the root of the Puritan view of foreign nations. In terms of their anxiety for the condition of the professors of true religion, the Puritans enunciated, although in no single comprehensive statement, a foreign policy that was often not in accord with the actual policies of the English government.

England as Israel

Because England was a part of the Church and because the Puritan view of foreign nations was based upon a concern for that Church, the Puritan view of foreign nations reflected a Puritan view of England. Hence, the Puritans did not just see a France, a Netherlands, or a Spain in the light of their religious outlook; to some extent they also saw their England mirrored in those nations and in the European struggle. The war compelled the Puritans to adopt religiously motivated attitudes toward the contestants, and those Puritan attitudes revealed ideals by which England, too, could be seen and judged. However, the England that was reflected in the Puritan views of foreign nations can best be understood if it is interpreted in relation to a Puritan image that provided the fundamental historical metaphor: the image of England as Israel.[1]

All peoples probably think of themselves as somehow standing in a special relationship to the divine. The Roman Catholic calendar of saints had offered identifying relationships to professions, crafts, cities, dynasties. Everywhere it triumphed, the Reformation destroyed the cults of those saints, but in England, where Reformation bore the Tudor impress, England with its monarch could provide the new boundaries for identification with divine power. Exaltations of Elizabeth and the exhortations of Caroline divines were one focus of identification. Another focus was England itself. Would Henry V

1. It should be kept in mind that this brief presentation of the Puritan image of England as Israel is not intended to be a full-scale interpretation. It is offered here in order to place the Puritan views of foreign nations and the reflections of those views on England in the framework of an important metaphor of historical perception. Vicars, *Englands Hallelu-jah,* is perhaps the best example of this metaphor. For background see Haller, *Foxe's Book of Martyrs and the Elect Nation,* 140–186, 224–250.

fully have understood *Henry V*? "God is English" — in Aylmer's famous marginal comment — would have been very odd earlier; its contemporary uniqueness was its terseness, not its sentiment. Although the definitions were not always religious, Protestantism helped to define an English nation. If God were English, England was God's. England was the elect nation, and Englishmen drew the parallels between the election of their nation and the election of Israel.

The English Puritans in the seventeenth century shared that metaphor and fully elaborated it. Their formulation is important to an understanding of their view of England's position in relation to foreign nations and the ways in which attitudes toward foreign nations reflected a view of England. For in seeing England as a chosen nation, the Puritans necessarily judged England by its performance of the duties imposed on it by its divine election. England was chosen to be another Israel; but like Israel, the Puritans perceived, England neither always acted in accord with the mission implicit to its calling nor always responded with gratitude for the blessings and mercies it enjoyed.

Nevertheless, the Puritan approach to the chosen but sinful Israel that was England was fundamentally optimistic. For, however corrupted the nation was, England remained a sanctuary of the true religion; and for the sake of that religion the divine wrath, no matter how harshly it was levied, was meant to be the means of purging the chosen people of their corruptions in order wholly to restore them to their God. Thus, to the Puritans even the heaviest scourgings of England were for the good; such punishments, although certainly merited by England's transgressions, were really another example of God's care for the chosen nation.[2] But to enjoy the return of the Lord to England, the English must, of course, cast off their sins and humble themselves with fasts

2. *Winthrop Papers,* II, 91–92; Leighton, *Speculum Belli sacri,* 307–308.

and prayers. Only by returning to its covenant with God could England regain the blessings so lavishly bestowed upon a favored people.[3] As a consequence of their certainty in God's care for England, the Puritans could only be impatient with impediments to England's full restoration to God's favor; their zeal on this point was clearly proclaimed: "Oh that wee were like Israel in Judges, who went to God the second time, humbling themselves and offering burnt-offerings and peace-offerings, whereupon the Lord gave their enemies into their hands. So if we would humble our selves and kill our sinnes, our enemies should quickly loose what they have got, and pay full deerly for all costs and damages."[4]

The Mirror of England

To the English Puritans the most important visible sign of the election of their nation was the presence of the true religion in England. Their religious nationalism did not conflict with their religious universalism, for the Puritans knew that the true religion did not abide exclusively in England: the Reformed were also in Europe, where they were sometimes politically gathered and sometimes dispersed among heathens. But wherever they were, their essentially similar beliefs bound them in a spiritual communion with the English Israel. Thus, while the Puritans held an image of England as Israel, they also considered the religious brethren in foreign lands as parts of the chosen people, chosen because of their covenant with God to serve as a holy people. So it was that in other lands there were, for the Puritans, parts of the whole Church; and in those parts England, which was another part,

3. *Commons Debates 1629*, 16; Leighton, *Speculum Belli sacri*, 208; Hampton, *A Proclamation of Warre*, 37–43.
4. Leighton, *Speculum Belli sacri*, 208.

could see ideals by which the English part could be measured.

Ideals of good and evil were present in the Europe of the Thirty Years' War, but it must not be forgotten that the ideals the Puritans beheld on the continent were embodied in the peoples and countries which were engaged in a titanic struggle. The religious brethren could not be viewed outside the context of the war; because they were involved, the Church and all of Israel were involved. The English Puritans were fully aware of this involvement, which to them took on the appearance of an Armageddon, for everywhere the holy people were at war with Antichrist. Ideals of good and evil confronted each other in that clash. The evil was represented by perfect evil, Romish Spain and its minions; the good, on the other hand, was represented by imperfect earthly good, the Reformed brethren burdened with their corruptions. Even in the necessarily imperfect good which was embodied in the professors of true religion, certain facets of the ideal of perfect good were observable. From those ideals of good and evil — ideals which can be abstracted from the Puritan views of foreign nations — the Puritans were also able to judge England; for England, as a part of the imperfectly good holy people, was mirrored by the ideals displayed within the context of an almost apocalyptic vision of the Thirty Years' War.

That England and especially the faults of England were reflected in the Puritan views of foreign countries is understandable. In any consideration of a foreign land there is a tendency to make a comparison with the homeland. The Puritans often framed the relationship between observer and observed as a series of negative identifications. The qualities admired in another country are often qualities that are desired in the country of the observer, or the problems of another people may serve as an example, warning, or solution for problems facing the observer's countrymen. In some of the European nations the Puritans saw qualities that they felt

England would be wise to emulate. Moreover, the Puritans observed difficulties abroad from which England could obtain valuable examples and even warnings. The qualities and problems of the foreign nations were not only aspects of Puritan ideals, they were also guides for the English on the internal ordering of England and the external posture expected of an elected nation.

The internal fault of most concern to the English Puritans was the impure condition of religion in England. Assured by past history and present example that God had chosen their nation for special favor, the Puritans could not fail to be anxious about the decayed state of God's greatest gift to the nation. Of the several impurities that marred religion in England, the most dangerous were the twin perils of Arminianism and Roman Catholicism, which in Puritan eyes were different forms of the same evil antagonist. Arminianism was nothing less than dissembling Romanism striving to corrupt the Church from within. Englishmen had only to look at the strife Arminianism had raised in the Netherlands in order to understand what it meant in England; and from the example of Dutch success and prosperity after the suppression of the heretics, the English could learn what must be done to preserve England and the true religion from the treacherous designs of the Arminian clergy. Nor was there a scarcity of examples to hinder England from discovering the hatred that papists bore to all believers of the Reformed religion. In France rabid papists, led by the pro-Spanish Jesuits, were to blame for misleading Louis XIII into persecuting and attacking his loyal Huguenot subjects. In Germany the religious brethren had been exiled or slaughtered because of warfare which had been provoked by Jesuit trickery to advance Romanism; as a result of popish enmity, an English Princess and her family had been driven out of Bohemia and the Palatinate to become homeless exiles. Yet, England tolerated recusancy and permitted Romish priests, even Jesuits, to roam the land, practice their faith, and gain converts to a cause committed to the destruction of true religion in England. To the Puritans the events across the sea were meant as revelation to England of the threat offered to that religion which above all marked the nation as one chosen by God. To ignore the examples in foreign nations — examples that had counterparts in England — was to hazard England's faith and election.

The foolish toleration of Arminianism and popery was a dangerous matter, but it was not the only English religious impurity offensive to God. In daily life and in religious performances, the English all too often acted in disregard of what the Puritans conceived to be the commandments of true religion. Here, too, the Puritans found examples and warnings for England in the practices and events in foreign nations. Whereas the Dutch humbled themselves with public fasts and prayers, whereas Gustavus Adolphus prayed for divine assistance and gave thanksgiving for it, England remained an arrogant nation, ungrateful to its God. While the Dutch were preserving their land and enlarging their commerce and while Gustavus Adolphus was gaining victories and glory, the Puritans beheld the melancholy position of England: trade suffering, the nation ill-defended, honor and resources lost in disastrous ventures. England would not humble itself before a generous God, and so England was made weak and contemptible before the nations of the world.

At least a partial cause of the impurity of life and religion in England was the failure of the English to hearken to the godly preachers who labored to recall Israel to its duties. This English fault was paralleled on the continent, where the Puritans marked the plight of the religious brethren in the Palatinate. There the Protestants had been preserved as long as their faithful ministers were among them, but now they were tortured, pillaged, persecuted, and driven from their homes. It was one of God's great favors to England to have furnished it with learned and godly preachers to be the means of its reconciliation and salvation; however, the Puritans felt that too few of their countrymen answered the call of God's messengers to reform sinful lives and cleanse the Church of its impurities. Instead, England allowed the false-hearted prelates to lead the nation into worse corruptions and, equally wrong, permitted the honest preachers to be hounded by those prelates. So far England had not been made to feel the sufferings of the Palatinate, although warnings in the form of plagues and famine had been plentiful; but if the prelates were ever to complete their task of silencing the preaching of God's true word in England then England could certainly expect to suffer.

Without the guidance of honest preachers, England would not be able to correct the other internal faults which were revealed in the light of examples from foreign nations. Until England followed the advice of wise counsellors and rid itself of sinfulness, ingratitude, and the internal enemies, papists and Arminians, England could not reach the ideals of a holy nation and would not be deserving of its election. Unless the English Israel learned from the vices and virtues, rewards and punishments, examples and warnings observable in other nations, England would not order its house in accord with the ideal ordering that was necessary for it to become a perfected nation wholly devoted to God in the pure observance of true religion. Furthermore, the ordering of England to a set of internal ideals was thought to be necessary so that the country could assume its rightful place in the world external to England — a world where the Church was engaged in the apocalyptic struggle with Antichrist. England, an Israel chosen and preserved by God, could not remain aloof from the battle, for the battle was God's and England was God's.

To the English Puritans the war in Europe presented a set of ideals by which the performance of England in the world could be judged. Oversimplified, it could express a political Manichaeism, in which the essentially evil world was the arena of conflict between good and evil, in which the saints battled for God where evil was more worldly real than good. Applied to nations, this simplified dualism could degenerate into "God with us," or "our country, right or wrong," but it equally could become "our country, when it is right." Puritanism provided a common source for both stances.

Within the setting of the Thirty Years' War, the Puritan view of foreign nations was a vision of Armageddon. Of course, the Puritans were not so naive as to approach every situation created by the war as if it were a clear instance of the ideal good opposed to the ideal evil. Such an approach too often would have failed to comprehend any reality at all, and a simplistic view which ignored the complex realities would have forced the Puritans to reject the utility of France and perhaps to adopt no view at all toward the Netherlands. On the contrary, within the context of the war, France and the Netherlands were both accepted into the ideal of the good. Nevertheless, this Puritan acceptance of imperfect nations was not a contradiction of Puritan idealism, for it should be remembered that the Puritans saw no nations as embodying perfect good. They saw instead the embodiment of perfect evil in the world, and, opposed to that perfect evil, the nations that imperfectly represented the presence of or protection for the perfect good that was the Church. For underlying all the Puritan attitudes to foreign nations was the Puritan concern for the Church. That fundamental concern informed the Puritan opinions so that imperfectly good nations, by securing the Church against the assaults of perfect evil, represented a greater good than they actually were. Thus, the reality of the war was raised to a cosmic plane. In terms of the ideals involved, the war was more than a savage blood-letting, it was Armageddon where the nations were tested — where England, too, was tested.

On the side of evil there was the easily identifiable antagonist. Spain was perfect evil. In the Puritans' picture of Spain as the army of Antichrist, there was no mixture of good; if there had been no Spain, they would have had to invent one. Its Romish religion marked its antagonism to God; its persecutions of God's children demonstrated its hatred of the true religion. Moreover, Spanish cruelty, inherent in the Spanish race, further separated the Spaniard from other people. Wherever the Puritans looked, they saw the alien Spaniard performing his antichristian labors. By means of subversion, trickery, and military assault, Spain sought the fulfillment of its design to seize the world, for the legions of Antichrist were largely interested in the increase of their temporalities. Knowing they were denied the other, they lusted for the ownership of this world. The Puritans, however, would not willingly concede to Spain's desire for universal monarchy. In the temporal sphere the Spaniard held the advantage, for here perfect evil could exist where, perhaps, perfect good was impossible; but the scattered elect, although they were not free of temporal corruptions, must stand against the cunning and ruthless embodiment of perfect evil that was Spain.

The force that contested Armageddon with the army of Antichrist was the force of the Protestants. Nowhere were they perfect, but as they fought under religion's banner they fought in the cause of an ideal good. In Germany, in the United Provinces, in the Huguenots of France, and in the King of Sweden, the cause of the Church was represented by imperfect men and imperfect institutions, but the cause for which they fought was perfect good. England, as the Puritans saw it, was naturally a part of the opposition to Antichrist, and England ought to have been in the forefront of the hosts of the godly. Not even the impurities of England could completely disguise its real character as a chosen nation, nor did the existence of some impurities distinguish England from the other Protestants. The Puritans had no doubts about which side England was required to take; yet when battle was joined, there was not much in the facts of English action to justify a Puritan belief that England was performing its duty to the cause of God.[5]

When the contestants were met in the course of battle, then England was tested by its deeds, deeds which in fact gave more pain than satisfaction to the Puritans. Protestantism suffered defeats in Germany, and the religious brethren there were subjected to horrible brutalities of body, to destruction of their property, and, more cruelly, to the loss of the comforts of their faith. The defeat and exile of royal English blood made the afflictions of the German brethren a special dishonor to England. But England's King, the father of the homeless Princess, dallied in negotiations with the tormentors of the German Protestants. When the French King, ill-advised by pro-Spanish traitors around him, persecuted and attacked the French Protestants, England, instead of relieving the suffering brethren, became the means of their defeat. To the Puritans it appeared that whenever the battle with Antichrist was going against the professors of true religion, England had a hand in their losses and sufferings. It was surely not the part expected of a chosen nation.

Although the Puritans rejoiced when Protestant arms were victorious, they found little reason to rejoice in the national share of England in those victories. True, Englishmen sometimes served as soldiers in the Dutch or Swedish armies, but

5. Walzer's formula that the analogue to crusade is revolution when nation replaces Christendom is limiting. The concepts of the crusading nation and the reforming of the nation were concurrent and related in seventeenth-century England. Walzer, *The Revolution of the Saints,* 270 (and see also 281–283, 291–293).

the English government also permitted recruitment of men for Spanish or Imperial service and allowed Spain to purchase English ordnance. The Puritans realized that the participation of a few Englishmen was inadequate help for Protestantism while England's neutrality was injuring the engaged Protestant nations. Nor did the actions of some English individuals represent England's engagement in the battle. When the Dutch on land and sea defended themselves or pushed the attack against Spain, they did so without the assistance of their English brethren; when Gustavus Adolphus landed to rescue the afflicted Church and to win victories over the forces of evil, no English ally joined him in the rescue nor shared in any of his glory. England, although an elected sanctuary, remained outside the struggle in which the Church contested with Antichrist for the world. Thus, when the Protestant cause was victorious, the Puritans experienced the shame of knowing that their English Israel could claim no share in the triumph.

Ultimate victory at Armageddon was assured to the side fighting for the cause of God's Church. The Antichrist was foredoomed to defeat. Although the Protestants suffered temporary defeats and the scorn of their enemy, the Puritans maintained a belief that those defeats would pass; the professors of true religion would not sustain permanent loss. But when the enemy was finally crushed, it would never be restored; the destruction of Antichrist would be final. Assured by their fervent belief that ultimate victory must come to the people of God, the Puritans were able to retain some particle of hope throughout the darkest times when Antichrist was everywhere victorious. It was because of their faith in the ordained outcome of the war that the English Puritans could offer comfort to the distressed religious brethren. The apocalyptic context, the certainty of victory, and the hopeful counsel were easily recognizable elements when Alexander

Leighton addressed words of comfort to the conquered brethren: "The fourth ground of your hope is from the enemie with whom you have to deale; namely, the beast, the Dragon, and the false Prophet, whose ruine the Lord of hoasts hath vowed and determined. It is a great advantage to know our enemies, but a greater incouragment to know that our enemies are Gods enemies, and God their enemie; so they cannot stand. What your enemies are, and what attempts they shall make, and how certainely, and suddenly they shall fall it is cleare in the Revelations."[6] The ideal good that was the Church would endure and in the end would triumph over its enemies. God had willed the victory.

Although the Puritans were certain of the victory, they could not be certain where England would stand at the final reckoning with the legions of Antichrist. In so many ways England acted not as an elected country but as if it were outside or even opposed to the Church standing against its historical enemy. If England would not fight in the contest of ideals, then England was not fulfilling its obligations to God. The Puritans saw England failing to succour the persecuted brethren, failing to attend the battle; and because of those failures they feared that England would not be counted on the side of God at Armageddon. To the Puritans the paramount danger to England was not that England was opening itself to Spanish attack by failing the religious brethren, for Spain could merely physically injure England; moreover, Spain, inasmuch as it was the representative of Antichrist, was inevitably doomed to destruction. To the Puritans England's greatest peril was that it was denying its allegiance to the ideal of the good by not allying itself with the cause of the Church; and this denial was also a denial of the God

6. Leighton, *Speculum Belli sacri*, 304–305. See also William Haller, *Liberty and Reformation in the Puritan Revolution* (New York, 1955), 47–48. Haller credits the influence of Foxe in the formation of this Puritan concept.

who had elected and preserved England. Envisioning the Thirty Years' War as Armageddon, the English Puritans knew it was the battle between good and evil — the battle in which the fate of nations would be decided. With the outcome of the battle foretold, a nation would be judged by its place on that battleground. The nations not joined in the inevitable triumph were destined to suffer to the utmost the divine wrath. In the view of the English Puritans their country could not be favorably judged in terms of the ideals observable in the great clash between good and evil. The England mirrored in the war was not an England that could be hopeful of deliverance from wrath, for at Armageddon England was denying its God.

The Thirty Years' War, considered as the apocalyptic battle between ideals of good and evil, was itself an ideal by which the performance of England was judged. But for the English Puritans the external testing of England also implied a testing of Englishmen. By an Englishman's responses to the conflict in Europe, an Englishman was known. Inasmuch as the conflict of nations was also seen as a conflict of ideals, the attitude of an individual toward the nations involved in the war was an attitude expressive of that individual's commitment to the ideals. Thus, loyalty to the ideal of Protestantism fully engaged in opposition to the Antichrist was the mark of the true believer and the true patriot. The truly patriotic Englishman could not want England to suffer the fullness of divine retribution; yet that chastisement of England was assured unless England abandoned its ungrateful ways. To persuade God of England's place among those nations to be delivered at Armageddon, the nation had to demmonstrate its worthiness by demonstrating its loyalty to God's embattled Church. This it could do by assisting those nations already fighting in the war. Therefore, the Puritans saw an individual's attitudes to foreign nations as evidence of that individual's concern for the salvation of England. A good Englishman must also be a good Protestant, and a good Protestant was one who was concerned about the condition of embattled Protestantism.

The reflection within England of the external ideals revealed by the European conflict was manifested in two recurrent themes of Puritan response: the use of the glorious Elizabethan past and the use of foreign nations as shibboleths. Both served the Puritans as means of identification, for true and false Englishmen could be distinguished by the application of those tests from the past and present.

To almost every question of foreign policy in this period, the Puritans were able to apply an Elizabethan precedent. Elizabeth had actively supported the Dutch with men and money. In France, the Puritans noted, Elizabeth had served as a peacemaker, healing the divisions in that country in order that a united France might repel the incursions of Spanish power. By these means the great Queen had secured friends for England, and she was therefore able to withstand the assaults of Spain. Furthermore, Elizabeth did not keep the nation inactive by depending upon others to fight for it, nor did she remain merely defensive, restricting the nation simply to reactions to Spanish attacks. Instead, she loosed against the Spanish lifelines her sea dogs, who became now a pantheon of heroes for the Puritans. Even the Elizabethan tactic merited praise, for the Puritans recalled that she had relied upon England's most effective arm, its navy, and had employed it in such a way that not only was the enemy severely injured but, as they remembered it, England reaped great profits from the capture of Spain's basic strength, the precious metals of the Americas.

All these Elizabethan policies were recalled and applauded by the English Puritans, but at the root of their praise was their view of England's relations to foreign nations in their own time. In their picture of the glorious past, what they saw was an England clearly committed to the battle against Spain. Under Elizabeth, England had forthrightly stood at the side of the religious brethren, aiding them in fighting the common enemy; and when England had fought for religion, England had been the honored leader of the cause, a leader glorious in victory, a nation happy, successful, and prosperous. For when England warred in God's cause, God blessed the land and the people. Because England had been so blessed in Elizabeth's reign, the Puritans of a later generation looked to her age for criteria of performance. They saw their England faced with what they thought were the very problems and situations which had faced Elizabethan England, and they naturally believed that the methods, as well as the general policy of supporting Protestantism, were still applicable. In Parliament attention to the duplication of Elizabethan methods became almost a fixation with some members, and the stubbornness of their adherence was one factor in the foreign policy disagreements which often divided King and Parliament. The significance of this Puritan identification with the past actions of England was that, seeing in the past the same problems, and the solutions to those problems, the Puritans were provided with yet another standard by which to gauge the present performance of England. Their views on the position of England were confirmed in past experience, while their opponents, when not charged with treachery, were at best considered as the advocates of untried policies, policies unsanctified by Elizabethan precedent. The Puritans, on the contrary, urged an almost rigid loyalty to the ways of Elizabeth; by identifying themselves with her ways, they were proclaiming England's place in the war of their time, the war to end time.

Allegiance to the heroic past was only one criterion used to distinguish Englishmen; the other involved the use of foreign nations as tests of loyalty. Issues of foreign policy were turned into shibboleths with which the Puritans were able to know the good from the false Englishman. The most interesting of the shibboleths was the Palatinate, which endured as a shibboleth long after it had lost meaning as a European political reality. Undoubtedly the popularity of Elizabeth of Bohemia contributed to this use, but the greater physical separation of the Palatinate from England probably was a factor in the facility with which it became a symbol. Profuse demonstrations of honor to Elizabeth of Bohemia, a certainty regarding the justice of the Elector Palatine's case, and a desire to have England effect the restoration of his territories were the attitudes the Puritans expected of loyal Englishmen. Papists and cryptopapists, men whose real loyalties were to Spain, were marked by their disrespect for the English Princess, their questioning of the Elector's rights, and their failure to work for his return.

The Puritan shibboleths regarding France and the United Provinces were similar. The traitor to England fastened upon every impediment to England's friendship with the French and Dutch; he magnified and dwelt upon every jarring incident in order that England might sever itself from those allies. The patriot was known by his favorable attitude toward the Netherlands and his willingness to weigh carefully all conflicts between the Dutch and English. As for France, the true Englishman favored a peacefully united France so that the Huguenots could enjoy some freedom and the great strength of France could be used against Spain. In both cases the essential identification was with the cause of religion as it stood assaulted by Spain.

Finally, an Englishman's view of Spain was a critical means of separating patriots from traitors. The patriot recognized Spain as the singular enemy to religion and England; only if he treated with the sword would he treat with the Spanish Antichrist. He knew that no mercy could be expected from

155

the Spaniard, who was by nature committed to seek by any means the domination of the world for the Spanish crown and the Roman religion. At best, Englishmen who accepted any negotiations with Spain were dupes; often they were denounced for being in the Spanish pay or owing their real allegiance to Spain. Inasmuch as everything Spain stood for was in clear opposition to English interests — interests of English safety from Spanish conquest and of England's preservation from divine wrath — anyone laboring for a policy other than one of forthright opposition to Spain was, in truth, seeking Spain's benefit and England's destruction. To listen to Spain was to heed the voice of evil. Thus, an Englishman who urged any accommodation with Spain was not just offering a different foreign policy, he was suggesting that England tolerate Antichrist. His suggestion marked him as a dangerous traitor to the nation; he had incorrectly pronounced a Puritan shibboleth — Spain.

Through their demands that England should adhere to a tradition-sanctified policy and through their employment of foreign nations as shibboleths, the English Puritans' views of other nations became touchstones of the individual Englishman's qualities as a true Protestant Englishman. Attitudes on English foreign policy were not simply responses to foreign events; they were also measurable indicators of an attitude toward England. The Puritan held an ideal picture of England: a nation elected to be another Israel, a holy people devoted to the pure performance of religion. In the real world, however, England was not pure, and one of its greatest sins was that it did not take its position in the battle against the antichristian Spaniard. The ideal and the real were in conflict — a conflict that focused on the views of individual Englishmen; for an Englishman's attitude toward foreign nations was also his statement about the place of England at Armageddon.

The heaviest responsibility for securing England's place on the great battleground rested upon those who bore office. Kings and ministers were given charge over the people to lead them aright. If England was failing its obligations to the cause of religion, much of the guilt must be the burden of the individuals who governed. Until his assassination, Buckingham was the most obvious figure to be blamed for not leading the nation in accord with its proper mission, and he was popular only when his policies toward Spain briefly coincided with the Puritan stance. Laud, though less concerned with foreign affairs, was condemned for disloyalty because of a slight he was thought to have given the Electoral family. Nor was the crown untouched by the Puritan criticism that England's foreign policy was often dangerous and sinful. Usually, criticism of the King must be inferred from the lavish praise of Elizabeth of Bohemia or Gustavus Adolphus, or from the expressions of regret about the death of Prince Henry, who was still being lamented twenty years later, or from allusions from the Bible, where there was no shortage of examples of kings who had failed to fight for God. James was denounced for acting the part of an unnatural father to his children who were fully engaged in the great battle. After a good beginning, Charles more than repeated his father's errors and, by Puritan standards, did not perform a single right deed for the cause of religion abroad. James, Charles, and their chief ministers failed the Puritan tests by which good Protestant Englishmen were revealed. Unlike England under Queen Elizabeth, England under James and Charles did not appear to be safely on the side of Protestantism at Armageddon.

From the standpoint of their fundamental concern for religion, the Puritans saw the struggle in Europe as the apocalyptic contest between ideals of good and evil — ideals which were represented by nations — and they therefore attached great importance to the stand taken by England. Ultimately confident that God would redeem the true Church and destroy its enemies, the Puritans' confidence in England as an elect nation could be shaken. They looked at their nation as they looked at their souls: they anxiously sought the signs of election, and their watchful moral bookkeeping included accounts of their England. In this time of crisis England was weighed and found wanting. The heaviest responsibility for England's failure must be borne by the monarchs who followed their own policies rather than God's. Against those royal policies the Puritans articulated an alternative that could be a challenge; their religious tests applied to the individual and the nation. Their view did not exclude the monarch, but neither did it require the monarch as the nation's singular focus and sole rallying point. They addressed themselves to kings, but they also appealed to an audience that, if not popular, was public. To the degree that their views — views which seemed to be winning a larger public acceptance — differed from the royal policies, the English Puritans were further alienated from the government of England as it was.

The Thirty Years' War had been but a decade old when John Preston, speaking of the distressed brethren abroad, directly addressed to Charles a warning that can stand as epitome and prophecy: "For if any be an impediment, nay if any doe not doe their best, I pronounce this in the Name of the most true God, that shall make it good sooner or later, they and their houses shall perish . . ." [7]

7. Preston, *The New Life,* in *Sermons Preached Before his Majestie,* 53.

Bibliography

Index

Bibliography

PRIMARY SOURCES

Unpublished Manuscripts

Folger MS V.a. 24, ca. 1620. "In what lamentable estate . . ." Folger
   Shakespeare Library.
Great Britain. State Papers Domestic, James I. Public Record Office.
Great Britain. State Papers Domestic, Charles I. Public Record Office.
The Gurney Manuscript. "Parliament Debates 1624." Typescript.
"The Nicholas Parliament Diary of 1624." Typescript.
"The Parliament Diary of Sir Walter Earle for 1624." Typescript.
The Winchilsea Manuscript. "Parliament Diary of John Pym for 1624."
   Typescript.

Published Works

When appropriate, the *STC* number of each work is given after its
title.

Ball, Thomas. *The Life of the Renowned Doctor Preston.* E. W. Harcourt, ed. Oxford, 1885.
Barnes, Thomas. *Vox Belli, Or An Alarum To Warre.* 1478. London,
   1626.

Birch, Thomas. *The Court and Times of Charles the First.* 2 vols. London, 1848.

Birch, Thomas. *The Court and Times of James the First.* 2 vols. London, 1848.

Bowyer, Robert, and Henry Elsing. *Notes of the Debates in the House of Lords . . . A. D. 1621, 1625, 1628.* Frances Helen Relf, ed. Camden Society, 3d ser., XLII. London, 1929.

Bridge, William. *The true Souldiers Convoy. A Sermon preached upon the xvjth day of May 1640, upon a prayer day, for the Princes good successe in going forth to warre.* 3732. Rotterdam, 1640.

Br[inckmair], L. *The Warnings of Germany by Wonderfvll Signes, and strange Prodigies seene in divers parts of that Countrye betweene the Yeare 1618 and 1638 Together with a briefe relation of the miserable Events which ensued.* 3759. London, 1638.

B[urges], J[ohn]. *Certaine letters declaring in part the passage of affaires in the Palatinate.* 1037. Amsterdam, 1621.

Burton, Henry. *For God, and the King. The Summe of Two Sermons Preached on the fifth of November last in St. Matthewes Friday-Streete.* 4141. N. p., 1636.

Chamberlain, John. *The Letters of John Chamberlain.* Edited with an introduction by Norman E. McClure. Memoirs of the American Philosophical Society, XII, part II. Philadelphia, 1939.

Clarke, Thomas. *The Popes deadly Wound: Tending to resolve all men, in the Chiefe and principall Points now in controversie betweene the Papists and Us.* 5364. London, 1621.

Commons Debates for 1621. Wallace Notestein, Frances Helen Relf, and Hartley Simpson, eds. 7 vols. New Haven, 1935.

Commons Debates for 1629. Wallace Notestein and Frances Helen Relf, eds. Minneapolis, 1921.

Cotton, John. *Gods Promise To His Plantation.* 5854. London, 1630.

[Cotton, Sir Robert Bruce]. *The Danger wherein the Kingdome now standeth, & the Remedie.* 5863. N. p., 1628.

C[rashaw], W[illiam]. *The Fatall Vesper, or A True and Punctuall Relation of that lamentable and fearefull accident, hapning on Sunday in the afternoone being the 26. of October last, by the fall of a roome in the Black-Friers in which were assembled many people at a Sermon, which was to be preached by Father Drurie a Jesuite.* 6015. London, 1623.

Debates in the House of Commons in 1625. S. R. Gardiner, ed. Camden Society, n.s., VI. Westminster, 1873.

D'Ewes, Sir Simonds. *The Autobiography and Correspondence of Sir Simonds D'Ewes, Bart., during the reigns of James I. and Charles I.* J. O. Halliwell, ed. 2 vols. London, 1845.

Divine and Politike Observations . . . Upon Some Lines in the speech of the Ar. B. of Canterbury, pronounced in the Starre-Chamber upon 14. June, 1637. 15309. Amsterdam, 1638.

Dyke, Jeremiah. *Good Conscience: Or A Treatise Shewing the Nature, Meanes, Marks, Benefit, and Necessity thereof.* 7415. London, 1624.

—— *A Sermon Preached at the Publicke Fast. To The Commons House of Parliament. April 5th 1628.* 7424. London, 1628.

Eliot, Sir John. *An Apology for Socrates and Negotium Posterorum.* A. B. Grosart, ed. 2 vols. Printed for Earl St. Germains and Private Circulation Only. London, 1881.

—— *The Letter Book of Sir John Eliot, 1625–1632.* A. B. Grosart, ed. 2 vols. London, 1882.

Elsing, Henry. *Notes of the Debates in the House of Lords . . . 1621.* S. R. Gardiner, ed. Camden Society, CIII. Westminster, 1870.

—— *Notes of the Debates in the House of Lords . . . 1624 and 1626.* S. R. Gardiner, ed. Camden Society, n.s., XXIV. Westminster, 1879.

Evelyn, John. *The Diary of John Evelyn.* E. S. de Beer, ed. 6 vols. Oxford, 1955.

The Fairfax Correspondence. George W. Johnson, ed. 2 vols. London, 1848.

The Fortescue Papers. S. R. Gardiner, ed. Camden Society, n.s., I. Westminster, 1871.

Gallants, to Bohemia, Or let us to the Warres again. 3207. London, ca. 1632.

Garrard, Edmund. *The Countrie Gentleman Moderator: Collections of such intermarriages, as have beene betweene the Royall Lines of England and Spaine, since the Conquest . . . with divers reasons to moderate the Country peoples passions, feares, and expostulations, concerning the Prince his Royall Match and State affaires.* 11624. London, 1624.

Gataker, Thomas. *Certaine Sermons, First Preached, And After Published at severall times.* 11652. London, 1637. (A collection of twenty sermons and meditations, including *David's Remembrancer,* 1623, and *Noah His Obedience With the Ground of It,* 1623.)

—— *A Sparke Toward the Kindling of Sorrow for Sion.* 11675. London, 1621.

Gee, John. *The Foot out of the Snare.* 11702. London, 1624.

Goodwin, John. *The Saints interest in God, opened in severall sermons, preached Anniversarily upon the fifth of November.* 12031. London, 1640.

Gouge, William. *Gods Three Arrowes: Plague, Famine, Sword, In three Treatises.* 12116. London, 1631.

—— *The Saints Sacrifice: Or A Commentarie on the CXVI Psalme.* 12125. London, 1632.

Great Britain. *Calendar of State Papers, Domestic Series, of the Reign of Charles I.* Vols. I–XV. London, 1858–1877.

Great Britain. *Calendar of State Papers, Domestic Series, of the Reign of James I.* Vols. X, XI. London, 1858–1859.

Hampton, William. *A Proclamation of Warre from the Lord of Hosts, Or Englands warning by Israels ruine: Shewing the miseries like to ensue upon us by reason of Sinne and Securitie.* 12741. London, 1627.

Harleian Miscellany. W. Oldys, ed. 12 vols. London, 1808–1811.

Harley Letters and Papers. Historical Manuscripts Commission, Fourteenth Report, Appendix, Part II: *The Manuscripts of His Grace The Duke of Portland, preserved at Welbeck Abbey.* Vol. III. London, 1894.

Harrison, John. *A Short Relation of the departure of the high and mightie Prince Frederick King Elect of Bohemia; with his royall & vertous Ladie Elizabeth: And the thryse hopefull young Prince Henrie, from Heydelberg towards Prague, to receiuse the Crowne of that Kingdome.* 12859. Dort, 1619.

Hutchinson, Lucy. *Memoirs of the Life of Colonel Hutchinson.* Julius Hutchinson, ed., revised by C. H. Firth. 2 vols. London, 1885.

Hyde, Edward, Earl of Clarendon. *The History of the Rebellion and Civil Wars in England.* W. D. Macray, ed. 6 vols. Oxford, 1888.

An Information From The States Of the Kingdome of Scotland, to the Kingdome of England. 21917+. Amsterdam, 1640.

Jenison, Robert. *The Height of Israels Heathenish Idolatrie, In sacrificing their children to the Devill.* 14491. London, 1621.

—— *Newcastles Call, To her Neighbour and Sister Townes and Cities throughout the land, to take warning by her Sins and Sorrowes.* 14492. London, 1637.

The Last newes from Bohemia. 3208. N. p., 1620.

Leighton, Alexander. *An Appeal to the Parliament; Or Sions Plea against the Prelacie.* 15429. [Amsterdam?], 1628.

L[eighton], A[lexander]. *Speculum Belli sacri: or the Lookingglasse of the Holy War Wherein is discovered: The Evill of War. The Good of Warr. The Guide of War.* 15432. N. p., 1624.

Letters and Other Documents Illustrating the Relations between England and Germany at the Commencement of the Thirty Years' War. S. R. Gardiner, ed. Camden Society, XC. Westminster, 1865.

Letters and Other Documents Illustrating the Relations between England and Germany at the Commencement of the Thirty Years' War. S. R. Gardiner, ed. Camden Society, 2d ser., XCVIII. Westminster, 1868.

Lowther. *Notes in Parliament, 1626 and 1628.* Historical Manuscripts Commission, Thirteenth Report, Appendix, Part VII: *The Manuscripts of the Earl of Lonsdale at Lowther Castle.* London, 1893.

Ludlow, Edmund. *The Memoirs of Edmund Ludlow.* C. H. Firth, ed. 2 vols. Oxford, 1894.

M., A. *A Relation of the Passages of our English Companies from time to time since their first departure from England to the parts of Germanie and the united Provinces.* 17125. London, 1621.

Newes From Bohemia An Apologie Made by the States of the Kingdom of Bohemia, shewing the Reasons why those of the Reformed Religion were moved to take arms, for the defence of the King and themselves, especially against the dangerous sect of Jesuits . . . 3211. London, 1619.

O., S. *An Adioynder of Sundry other particular wicked plots and cruel, inhumane, perfidious, yea, unnatural practices of the Spaniards: Chiefly against the seventeen provinces of the Netherlands; yea, before they tooke up Armes.* 18757. N. p., 1624.

The Oxinden Letters, 1607–1642. Dorothy Gardiner, ed. London, 1933.

P., H. *Digitus Dei or Good Newes from Holland. Sent to the world . . . As also to all that have shot arrows agaynst Babels Brats, and wish well to Sion wheresoever.* 19066. Rotterdam, 1631.

The Present state of the affairs betwixt the Emperor and King of Bohemia. 10815. [London?], 1620.

Preston, John. *The Saints Qualifications.* Richard Sibbes and John Davenport, eds. 20264. London, 1633. (A posthumous collection, including *A Sermon Preached at a Generall Fast before the Commons-House of Parliament: the second of July, 1625.*)

———— *Sermons Preached Before his Majestie; and upon other speciall occassions.* 20270. London, 1630. (Five sermons published posthumously, including *The Pillar and Ground of Truth,* 1625, *The New Life,* 1628, and *A sensible Demonstration of the Deity.* 1627 [?].)

R., J. *The Spy Discovering the Danger of Arminian Heresie and Spanish Trecherie*. 20577. Strasburgh, 1628.

The reasons wh. compelled the states of Bohemia to reject the archiduke Ferdinand. 3212. Dort, 1619.

A Relation of a New League made by the Emperour of Germany, with other Princes, Potentates and States Catholicke, against the Enemies of the Roman Catholick-Religion, with the Names, of those Princes. 10817. N. p., 1626.

Rous, John. *Diary*. M. A. E. Green, ed. Camden Society, LXVI. London, 1856.

[Scott, Thomas?]. *The Interpreter Wherein three principall termes of State much mistaken by the vular are clearely unfolded*. 14115. N. p., 1622.

[Scott, Thomas]. *Sir Walter Rawleighs Ghost, or Englands Forewarner. Discovering a secret Consultation, newly holden in the Court of Spaine*. 22085. Utrecht, 1626.

Scott, Thomas. *The Workes of the Most Famous and Reverend Divine Mr. Thomas Scot*. 22064. Utrecht, 1624. (Houghton Library, Harvard University, lists its copy as one of two known copies of this collection of 24 tracts bound together with a preface and title page. The scarcity of this volume and the importance of Scott in this study make it necessary to list the individual items, which, although read from *The Workes,* are separate tracts with their own *STC* number.)

——— *The Belgicke Pismire: Stinging the slothfull Sleeper, and Awaking the Diligent to Fast, Watch, Pray; and Worke Out Their Owne Temporall and Eternall Salvation With Feare and Trembling*. 22069. London, 1622.

——— *The Belgick Souldier: Dedicated to the Parliament. Or, Warre was a Blessing*. 22072. Dort, 1624.

——— *Boanerges. Or The Humble Supplication Of The Ministers Of Scotland, To The High Court Of Parliament In England*. 3171. Edinburgh, 1624.

——— *A Briefe Information of the Affaires of the Palatinate*. 19126. N. p., 1624.

——— *Certaine Reasons and Arguments of Policie, Why the King of England should hereafter give over all further Treatie, and enter into warre with the Spaniard*. 22073. N. p., 1624.

—— *Digitus Dei.* 22075. N. p., 1623.

—— *Englands Joy, For Suppressing the Papists, and banishing the Priests and Jesuites.* 22076. N. p., 1624.

—— *An Experimentall Discoverie of Spanish Practises or The Counsell of a well-wishing Souldier, for the good of his Prince and State.* 22077. [London?], 1623.

—— *Newes from Pernassus. The Politicall Touchstone, Taken From Mount Pernassus: Whereon the Governments of the greatest Monarchies of the World are touched.* 22080. Helicon [Utrecht?], 1622.

—— *Robert Earle of Essex His Ghost, Sent from Elizian: To The Nobility, Gentry, And Communaltie Of England.* 22084. Paradise [London], 1624. (With a separate title page but with no separate *STC* number, a "Post Script" to this work follows it.)

—— *A Second Part of Spanish Practises. Or, A Relation Of More Particular wicked plots, and cruell, inhumane, perfidious, and unnaturall practises of the Spaniards.* 22105a. N. p., 1624.

—— *The Second Part of Vox Populi, or Gondomar appearing in the likenes of Matchiavell in a Spanish Parliament wherein are discovered his treacherous & subtile Practises To the ruine as well of England, as the Netherlandes.* 22104. Goricom, 1624.

—— *The Spaniards Perpetuall Designes To An Universall Monarchie.* 22086. [London?], 1624.

—— *A Speech Made In The Lower House of Parliament, By Sir Edward Cicell, Colonell.* 22088. London, 1624. (Although *STC* gives 1621 as the date, 1624 is printed on the pamphlet itself.)

—— *Symmachia: or, A True-Loves Knot. Tyed, Betwixt Great Britaine and the United Provinces, by the wisedome of King James, and the States Generall; the Kings of France, Denmarke, and Sweden, the Duke Savoy, with the States of Venice being Witnesses and Assistants. For the Weale and Peace of Christendome.* 22089. [Utrecht?, 1624?].

—— *A Tongue-Combat, Lately Happening Betweene two English Souldiers in the Tilt-boat of Gravesend, The One Going to Serve the King of Spaine, the other to serve the States Generall of the United Provinces. Wherein the Cause, Course, and Continuance of those Warres, is debated and declared.* 22091. London, 1623.

—— S.R.N.I. *Votivae Angliae: Or, The Desires And Wishes of England. Contained in a Patheticall Discourse, presented to the King on New-Yeares Day last.* 22093. Utrecht, 1624.

——— *Vox Coeli, or Newes From Heaven.* 22095. Elisium [Utrecht?], 1624.

——— *Vox Dei.* 22097. N. p., 1624.

——— *Vox Populi or Newes From Spayne, translated according to the Spanish coppie. Which may serve to forwarn both England and the United Provinces how farre to trust to Spanish pretences.* 22098. N. p., 1620.

——— *Vox Regis.* 22105. N. p., 1624. (The references in this pamphlet to the wrongs corrected by King and Parliament would appear to make the *STC* date of 1623 impossible.)

Sibbes, Richard. *The Bruised Reede, and Smoaking Flax.* 22479. London, 1630.

Somers Tracts. Sir Walter Scott, ed. 13 vols. London, 1809–1815.

Something Written by occasion of that fatall and memorable accident in the Blacke Friers on Sonday, being the 26. of October 1623 stilo antiquo, and the 5. of November stilo novo, or Roman. 3101. N. p., 1623.

The Swedish Discipline, Religious, Civile, And Military. The First Pare, in the Formes of Prayer daily used by those of the Swedish Nation, in the Armie. Together with two severall Prayers, uttered upon severall occasions by that pious King, which God immediately heard and granted him. 11790.5. London, 1632.

S.R.N.I. *See* Scott, Thomas.

Taylor, John. *A Friendly Farewell to all the noble Souldiers that goe out of Great Britaine unto Bohemia.* 23751. N. p., 1620.

Taylor, Thomas. *Christs Victorie over the Dragon: or Satans Downfall: Shewing the glorious Conquests of our Saviour for his poore Church, against the greatest Persecutions.* 23823. London, 1633.

T[aylor], T[homas]. *A Mappe of Rome: Lively Exhibiting Her Merciles Meeknes and cruell mercies to the Church of God. Preached in severall Sermons on occasion of the Gunpowder-Treason . . .* 23842. London, 1634. (First printed in 1619.)

Theol., Vincent. *The Lamentations of Germany. Wherein, As in a Glass, we may behold her miserable condition, and reade the woefull effects of sinne . . . and illustrated by Pictures the more to affect the Reader.* 24761. London, 1638

Troubles in Bohemia and other kingdomes procured by Jesuits. 3213. N. p., 1619.

A True Relation of the Uniust, Cruell, and Barbarous Proceedings against the English at Amboyna In the East-Indies by the Neatherlandish Governour and Councel there. 7451. London, 1624.

Vicars, John. Englands Hallelu-jah; or, Great Britaines retribution. 24697. London, 1631.

Wadsworth, James. The English Spanish Pilgrime. Or, A New Discoverie of Spanish Popery and Jesuiticall Stratagems. With the estate of the English Pentioners and Fugitives under the King of Spaines Dominions, and elsewhere at this present. 24926a. London, 1630.

Ward, Samuel. A Peace Offering To God For the Blessings we enjoy under his Majesties reigne, with a Thanksgiving for the Princes safe returne on Sunday the 5. of October. 1623. 25054. London, 1624.

Warwick, Sir Philip. Memoirs of the Reign of King Charles the First. Edinburgh, 1813.

[Watt, W.]. The Swedish Intelligencer. 23523. London, 1632.

Whitelock, Bulstrode. Memorials of the English Affairs from the Beginning of the Reign of Charles the First to the Happy Restoration of King Charles the Second. 4 vols. Oxford, 1853.

Wilkinson, Robert. The Stripping of Joseph, Or The crueltie of Brethren to a Brother . . . with a Consolatorie Epistle, to the English-East-India Companie, for their unsufferable wrongs susstayned in Amboyna, by the Dutch there. Published and presented unto them by Tho. Myriell. Pastor of Saint Stephens in Walbrooke. 25663. London, 1625.

Winthrop Papers. S. E. Morison et al., eds. 5 vols. Boston, 1929–1947.

Yonge, Walter. The Diary of Walter Yonge, Esq. from 1604 to 1628. George Roberts, ed. Camden Society, XLI. London, 1848.

SECONDARY WORKS

Aiken, W. A., and Henning, B. D. Conflict in Stuart England. Essays in honour of Wallace Notestein. London, 1960.

Carter, Charles H. The Secret Diplomacy of the Hapsburgs, 1598–1625. New York, 1964.

Collinson, Patrick. The Elizabethan Puritan Movement. London, 1967.

Davies, Godfrey. "Arminian versus Puritan in England, ca. 1620–1640," the Huntington Library Bulletin, No. 5 (April 1934), 157–179.

—— "English Political Sermons, 1603–1640," Huntington Library Quarterly, 3, no. 1 (October 1939), 1–22.

Davies, Horton. *The Worship of the English Puritans.* Glasgow, 1948.

Davis, Edward Louis. "The Revolution in English foreign policy, 1618–1624: a study in the growth of Puritan influence," unpub. diss. Harvard University, 1959.

Edmundson, George. *Anglo-Dutch Rivalry, 1600–1653.* Oxford, 1911.

Frank, Joseph. *The Beginnings of the English Newspaper 1620–1660.* Cambridge, Mass., 1961.

Gardiner, S. R. *History of England from the Accession of James I. to the Outbreak of the Civil War, 1603–1642.* New edition. 10 vols. London, 1893–1899.

George, Charles H. "Puritanism in History and Historiography," *Past and Present,* 41 (December 1968), 77–104.

George, Charles H., and Katherine George. *The Protestant Mind of the English Reformation, 1570–1640.* Princeton, 1961.

Geyl, Pieter. *The Netherlands in the Seventeenth Century.* Part One, 1609–1648. Revised and enlarged edition. New York, 1961.

Hall, Basil. "Puritanism: The Problem of Definition," *Studies in Church History,* II, 283–296. G. J. Cuming, ed., London, 1965.

Haller, William. *Foxe's Book of Martyrs and the Elect Nation.* London, 1963.

–––––– *Liberty and Reformation in the Puritan Revolution.* New York, 1955.

–––––– *The Rise of Puritanism.* New York, 1938.

Hill, Christopher. *Puritanism and Revolution: Studies in Interpretation of the English Revolution of the 17th Century.* London, 1958.

–––––– *Society and Puritanism in Pre-Revolutionary England.* New York, 1964.

Hulme, Harold. *The Life of Sir John Eliot.* New York, 1957.

Jordan, W. K. *The Development of Religious Toleration in England.* 4 vols. Cambridge, Mass., 1932–1940.

Levy, F. J. "The Making of Camden's *Britannia,*" *Bibliothèque d'Humanisme et Renaissance,* 26 (1964), 70–97.

Maclear, J. F. "The Influence of the Puritan Clergy on the House of Commons, 1625–1629," *Church History,* 14, no. 4 (December 1945), 272–289.

–––––– "Puritan Relations with Buckingham," *Huntington Library Quarterly,* 21, no. 2 (February 1958), 111–132.

Mitchell, William M. *The Rise of the Revolutionary Party in the English House of Commons, 1603–1629.* New York, 1957.

Mosse, George L. *The Holy Pretence: a Study in Christianity and Rea-*

son of State from William Perkins to John Winthrop. Oxford, 1957.

Newton, Lady. *The House of Lyme.* London, 1917.

A Short-Title Catalogue of Books Printed in England, Scotland, & Ireland and of English Books Printed Abroad, 1475–1640. A. W. Pollard and G. R. Redgrave, comps. 2 vols. London, 1926.

Walzer, Michael. *The Revolution of the Saints: A Study in the Origins of Radical Politics.* Cambridge, Mass., 1965.

Wedgwood, C. V. *The Thirty Years War.* London, 1957.

Willson, D. H. *The Privy Councillors in the House of Commons, 1604–1629.* Minneapolis, 1940.

Wright, L. B. "Propaganda against James I's 'Appeasement' of Spain," *Huntington Library Quarterly,* 6, no. 2 (February 1943), 149–172.

———— *Religion and Empire.* Chapel Hill, 1943.

Index

Goliath, 54
Gondomar, Count, 19, 49
Gouge, William, 7, 18, 41, 131
Greenland, 91
Grenville, Sir Richard, 47
Gunpowder Plot, 58, 60
Gustavus Adolphus, 7, 8, 125–138, 145, 148, 150, 157

Haller, William, 151n
Hapsburgs, 52, 57, 104, 126, 131; see also Austria; Ferdinand II; Spain
Hawkins, John, 47
Heath, Sir Robert, 88
Heidelberg, 41; see also Palatinate
Henri IV, 108, 109
Henrietta Maria, 107–111
Henry (Prince of Wales), 18, 107, 134, 137, 157
Henry V, 140
Henry V, 141
High Commission, 129
History, 3, 42, 100; see also Elizabeth I
Huguenots, 100, 101, 111–121, 126, 144, 148, 149; see also La Rochelle; Protestantism
Hus, John, 12
Hutchinson, Lucy, 42, 47, 111, 117–118

Indies, 91, 96
Infanta of Spain, see Spain, marriage
Israel, 28, 42, 60, 105, 118, 141, 143, 145; England as, 140–142, 146, 150, 156, 158
Italy, 106

James I, 2, 5, 9, 37, 39, 47, 49, 62, 65, 67, 69, 70, 74, 79, 115, 149, 157; fails to act for Palatinate, 12–22, 52–53; and Parliament, 23–31
Jenison, Robert, 77
Jerome of Prague, 12
Jesuits, see Roman Catholics
John George of Saxony, 15

La Rochelle, 9, 114, 118, 120, 121, 126; see also Huguenots; Ré
Laud, William (Archbishop), 6, 38–39, 42, 81, 116, 126, 157
Leighton, Alexander, 13, 15, 19, 28, 61, 69, 92, 93, 95, 110, 118
Leipzig, 130
Lincoln's Inn, 22
London, 101
Louis XIII, 106, 114–117, 126, 144, 149
Ludlow, Edmund, 111, 116, 118
Lutherans, 15, 132; see also Germany
Lutzen, battle of, 133

Magdeburg, sack of, 66, 127, 130
Manichaeism, political, 147
Mansfield, Count, 32
Mantua, 105
Marian persecutions, 66
Mary I, 67, 69
Milton, John, 1
Muscovy, 91
Myriell, Thomas, 86

Narrow Seas, 91
Nationalism, 1–2, 9, 120, 142; see also Patriotism
Navy, 33, 53, 56, 117, 153
Netherlands, see Dutch
Nethersole, Sir Francis, 33, 39
New England, 126
New World, 57n; see also Americas
News, see Publishing
Nordlingen, battle of, 5, 135, 136
Norrisses, the, 47

Oxford, 32

Palatinate, 8, 11–44, 45, 51–53, 65, 66, 75–76, 100–101, 113, 116, 123, 144, 145, 146; as symbol, 41–44, 155; see also Elizabeth of Bohemia; Frederick V; Germany
Pamphlets, see Publishing
Parliament, 4, 6, 22–37, 51–52, 54–56, 59, 61–63, 69, 75, 77–78, 93, 95, 101, 109–110, 113, 121, 124–126, 136, 154; privileges, 24, 27

Harvard Historical Studies

33. *Lewis George Vander Velde.* The Presbyterian Churches and the Federal Union, 1861–1869. 1932.

35. *Donald C. McKay.* The National Workshops: A Study in the French Revolution of 1848. 1933.

38. *Dwight Erwin Lee.* Great Britain and the Cyprus Convention Policy of 1878. 1934.

48. *Jack H. Hexter.* The Reign of King Pym. 1941.

58. *Charles C. Gillispie.* Genesis and Geology: A Study in the Relations of Scientific Thought, Natural Theology, and Social Opinion in Great Britain, 1790–1850. 1951.

62, 63. *John King Fairbank.* Trade and Diplomacy on the China Coast: The Opening of the Treaty Ports, 1842–1854. One-volume edition. 1953.

64. *Franklin L. Ford.* Robe and Sword: The Regrouping of the French Aristocracy after Louis XIV. 1953.

66. *Wallace Evan Davies.* Patriotism on Parade: The Story of Veterans' and Hereditary Organizations in America, 1783–1900. 1955.

67. *Harold Schwartz.* Samuel Gridley Howe: Social Reformer, 1801–1876. 1956.

69. *Stanley J. Stein.* Vassouras: A Brazilian Coffee County, 1850–1900. 1957.

71. *Ernest R. May.* The World War and American Isolation, 1914–1917. 1959.

72. *John B. Blake.* Public Health in the Town of Boston, 1630–1822. 1959.

73. *Benjamin W. Labaree.* Patriots and Partisans: The Merchants of Newburyport, 1764–1815. 1962.

74. *Alexander Sedgwick.* The Ralliement in French Politics, 1890–1898. 1965.

75. *E. Ann Pottinger.* Napoleon III and the German Crisis, 1865–1866. 1966.

76. *Walter Goffart.* The Le Mans Forgeries: A Chapter from the History of Church Property in the Ninth Century. 1966.

77. *Daniel P. Resnick.* The White Terror and the Political Reaction after Waterloo. 1966.

78. *Giles Constable.* The Letters of Peter the Venerable. 1967.

79. *Lloyd E. Eastman.* Throne and Mandarins: China's Search for a Policy during the Sino-French Controversy, 1880–1885. 1967.

80. *Allen J. Matusow.* Farm Policies and Politics in the Truman Years. 1967.

81. *Philip Charles Farwell Bankwitz.* Maxime Weygand and Civil-Military Relations in Modern France. 1967.

82. *Donald J. Wilcox.* The Development of Florentine Humanist Historiography in the Fifteenth Century. 1969.

83. *John W. Padberg, S.J.* Colleges in Controversy: The Jesuit Schools in France from Revival to Suppression, 1813–1880. 1969.

84. *Marvin Arthur Breslow.* A Mirror of England: English Puritan Views of Foreign Nations, 1618–1640. 1970.